memorize
SCRIPTURE

"The gospels show that Jesus Christ quoted scripture when undergoing the greatest crises of his life and ministry—like struggling against Satan or undergoing his death on the Cross. Yet many Catholics have never memorized a single verse. Jackie Angel has written a great book to help us learn to memorize scripture, and I urge every Catholic to get a copy!"

John Bergsma
Professor of Theology
Franciscan University of Steubenville

"At a time when so many thoughts and images clamor for the attention of our minds and hearts, Jackie Angel has put together a fantastic resource to help people of all ages be truly formed by sacred scripture, the Word of God. This book will surely help us put God first and restore peace to our minds and hearts. What a gift!"

Sarah Swafford
Speaker and author of *Gift and Grit* and *Emotional Virtue*

"Knowing scripture is essential for the Christian life. And memorizing sacred scripture is essential to allow God's Word to take root in our lives and shape our thoughts and actions. Jackie Angel has created a way of not only approaching God's Word but also of allowing the Word to take up residence in our hearts."

Fr. Mike Schmitz

memorize

SCRIPTURE

SIMPLE STEPS TO PRAY, PONDER, AND PRACTICE GOD'S WORD

JACKIE ANGEL

AVE MARIA PRESS AVE Notre Dame, Indiana

Nihil Obstat: Reverend Monsignor Michael Heintz, PhD
            Censor Librorum
Imprimatur: Most Reverend Kevin C. Rhoades
            Bishop of Fort Wayne–South Bend
            Given at Fort Wayne, Indiana, on October 22, 2024

Founded in 1865, Ave Maria Press is a ministry of the United States Province of Holy Cross.

www.avemariapress.com

Hardcover: ISBN-13 978-1-64680-389-7

E-book: ISBN-13 978-1-64680-390-3

Cover image © iStock / Getty Images Plus.

Cover and text design by Brianna Dombo.

Printed and bound in the United States of America.

Library of Congress Cataloging-in-Publication Data is available.

Let the word of Christ dwell in you
richly, as in all wisdom you teach
and admonish one another, singing
psalms, hymns, and spiritual songs
with gratitude in your hearts to God.

COLOSSIANS 3:16, NAB

Contents

INTRODUCTION

My Journey

"Let the word of Christ dwell in you richly" (Col 3:16, NAB). Let the word of Christ dwell in you. Let the word of Christ dwell. What a high calling! It's one I am still striving toward, and I've recently come to ponder, How can we possibly let the word of Christ dwell in us if we don't know the scriptures deeply in our hearts? And how can we know the scriptures deeply in our hearts if we don't read the Bible? You might be thinking, "Yeah, Jackie, you are a professional Catholic speaker and musician. You need to know scripture for those things!" Well, you're right, but I can also confidently tell you that aside from the professional aspect of using scripture, I use scripture daily in all areas of my life.

Let me explain. When I'm sitting on a plane and feel it accelerating during takeoff, I'll pray, "Keep me safe, O God" (Ps 16:1, NAB). Ditto when I get on the freeway, especially on the anxiety-inducing drive to downtown Dallas when other cars act like it's a NASCAR racetrack. Whenever I find myself in a time of desolation or in the desert of doubting my faith (or, when I was single, feeling that ache and longing for a spouse), I recite my favorite psalm:

Oh God, you are my God—for you I long! For you my body yearns; for you my soul thirsts, Like a land parched, lifeless, and without water. So I look to you in the sanctuary to see your power and glory. For your love is better than life.

PSALM 63, NAB

When I'm praying for someone, I recall the scriptures that tell me that faith moves mountains (Mt 17:20–21) and that we will receive what we ask for in faith (Mt 7:7–8). When I am in a tough stage in life (whether physically, mentally, financially, or with the kids), I recall that "God is faithful and will not let you be tried beyond your strength; but with the trial he will also provide a way out, so that you may be able to bear it" (1 Cor 10:13, NAB). And now that I have children who are learning to memorize scripture, we jovially put our names in 1 Corinthians 13 when someone is being sassy (including myself) and say, "Jackie is patient and kind; Jackie is not jealous or boastful" (especially when I know I'm not being patient or kind, it's very convicting!).

But this hasn't always been my reality. I didn't grow up memorizing scripture as a child, and I honestly didn't even open the Bible on my own terms until I was eighteen years old. While I had read scripture passages in youth group and at my friend's Protestant Bible study, I never read the Bible independently. I was intimidated by the size and complexity of the Bible, and I didn't have a clue where to begin. I wanted scripture to be relevant to my life in a practical way as a young adult, but I simply wasn't motivated enough to do anything about it. I heard scripture proclaimed every Sunday at Mass, so why should I put effort into hearing it more often? I was a well-behaved and obedient kid who abided (mostly) by the rules of my Catholic faith (at least the ones I knew), but I didn't have a personal relationship with Jesus. Although I attended Mass every Sunday, said grace before meals, said bedtime prayers, went to youth group (mostly for the social aspect), and otherwise did the bare minimum of being Catholic, I really didn't know what my faith taught or why it taught what it did. I had no clue that, right around the corner, a whole world was about to open up to me in my faith.

My journey with memorizing scripture began the summer before college when I applied to be a Young Apostle for a Steubenville Youth Conference in Tucson, Arizona. I had attended a weekend conference before (which I thought was pretty cool), but this time I was going to spend the week leading up to the conference with twenty-five other high school juniors and seniors (or recently graduated seniors) who wanted to help lead and serve the other two thousand high schoolers that would attend the weekend conference. I thought because I was a leader and high achiever in school, I would be a great leader in the Catholic realm. After all, I was president of my senior class, varsity volleyball captain, president of the French club, and valedictorian of my graduating class. Certainly, I could handle leading some teens through a weekend retreat. Oh, how foolish I was! During that week of Young Apostles, I encountered other Catholic teens who actually knew their faith, who were on fire with their love for God, and who were practically speaking a foreign language to me of Catholicism. It was humbling and exciting.

I had never heard of a Divine Mercy chaplet. Padre Pio, who? NFP—what is *that*? The Rosary? I only knew that there are Hail Marys and Our Fathers. I never realized that those prayers could be put together in an intentional meditation on the life of Christ. I had grown up Catholic, but that week was filled with firsts: the first time I went to daily Mass (seven days in a row!), the first time I heard the Church's teaching on contraception (which was quite a shock for me—I thought you could do whatever you wanted when you got married), the first time I met young men and women who were so pure-hearted and joyful and full of wisdom and knowledge about their faith and the Bible, the first time I fell in love with Jesus in the Eucharist (especially in the many opportunities to sit before him in adoration), and another big first—I started to memorize scripture.

That week we were asked to memorize two verses:

For freedom Christ set us free; so stand firm and do not submit again to the yoke of slavery.

GALATIANS 5:1, NAB

Present your bodies as a living sacrifice, holy and acceptable to God, which is your spiritual worship. Do not be conformed to this world but be transformed by the renewal of your mind, that you may prove what is the will of God, what is good and acceptable and perfect.

ROMANS 12:1–2

It has been more than twenty years since I first memorized those scriptures, and I still know them by heart. It was during this time of my life that I started learning some important tricks for my own memory. A group of missionaries taught us one of them: We would sit in a circle, and everyone would say one word from the verse we were trying to memorize. Then we would change seats and repeat. It was fun, and it really helped solidify those scriptures in my mind. After that week,

I began going to daily Mass, studying my faith by reading every Catholic book I could get my hands on, and opening up the Bible to not only read it but memorize it.

I remember having a Protestant friend in high school who participated in Bible competitions. For one competition he had to memorize all four chapters of Philippians, and he would be quizzed on it. Hearing this inspired me to set the goal of memorizing one scripture a week. As someone who was a theater kid since I was five years old and could memorize entire pages of a script, one scripture a week was *absolutely* doable. Really, my goal is still to memorize all of Romans 12 and maybe even all of Philippians. Our brains are amazing sponges, and even now, at "middle age," I don't want to lose that ability!

To begin memorizing scripture, I would page through the New Testament and find verses that pierced my heart so much that I wanted to learn them and keep them in my brain for future use—whether it was for my prayer life, for giving talks, for defending the faith, or to share with others. I would jot down a new verse on a sticky note and put it on my bathroom mirror so I could look at it every morning when getting ready for the day. I would also try to write it down as often as possible. At this point I was in college, so doodling while a professor was giving a lecture was a common thing for me.

As a volunteer for our middle and high school youth groups at my parish and as the president of the Newman

Club at my college, I was frequently giving thirty-minute talks on Jesus. Memorizing scripture was a massive aid in developing talks and giving them without notes. On my secular college campus, I wore Jesus T-shirts all the time, which would often lead to high fives from Protestant students. They were exceptionally friendly at first but would inevitably start grilling me when they found I was Catholic: Why do you confess your sins to a priest? Why do you ask saints to pray for you? Why do you treat Mary differently from any other woman? When I started reciting scripture in explanation of my answers, they were shocked that a Catholic even read the Bible, let alone memorized verses from it.

I was active in music ministry at my parish, and we were encouraged to sing the psalms verbatim rather than use settings that paraphrased them. So I started writing tons of psalm settings. And guess what? Because they are set to music, and music is a fantastic way to memorize, I know many of the psalms by heart because I sang them so often!

As you can see, there are multiple methods for committing scripture to memory. The purpose of this book is to provide a starting point and a program for a lifetime of memorizing scripture. Being a disciple of Jesus Christ is reason enough to "let the word of Christ dwell in you richly," because when you love someone, you want them to be a part of you—your heart, mind, body, and soul—but all the desire in the world can only get you so far. At some point, you need to take practical steps to internalize the Word of God. I pray that this book may be your guide as you discover how scripture comforts, convicts, teaches, and transforms us, because the Word isn't a dead thing; it is "living and active, sharper than any two-edged sword, piercing to the division of soul and spirit, of joints and marrow, and discerning the thoughts and intentions of the heart" (Heb 4:12).

How to Use This Book

I am so grateful you have chosen to pick up this book in hopes of knowing and loving the Word of God more deeply! I know that the thought of learning and memorizing passages from the Bible can be daunting because there is a lifetime worth of scriptures, and it often feels overwhelming with the thought of "Where do I even begin?" That's where this book comes in! Included in this book are some very foundational scriptures—many of which you have heard or seen over and over again—John 3:16, anyone?—which I have divided into themes over the course of a year.

These themes correspond to the monthly flow of the *Memorize Scripture* podcast. If you have a goal of memorizing one scripture a week for a year, you can start at the beginning of the book and just go through in order with the podcast. As I was going through the year and choosing the theme for each month, I wanted to start with foundational scriptures about God and his love. And then some months just made sense (i.e., Easter is usually in April, so I chose scriptures about rejoicing in the fourth month, and Advent is in December, so I chose scriptures about longing for God in the twelfth month). But you don't have to go chronologically—that's just an option if you want to spend a year memorizing scripture. But if a particular theme speaks to your heart, and you want to memorize scriptures pertaining to that theme, you can just jump to that chapter and begin there!

Each chapter includes a reflection on the theme of the month, a prayer, questions to ponder, and then scriptures to memorize and practice tips for memorizing. The first four scripture verses are the primary verses that we have memorized in the podcast. And then I have added additional alternative verses for the theme that you can also memorize if you so choose!

The scriptures are excerpted from the two most often used Catholic translations of the Bible—the *New American Bible* (which is heard/used at Mass) and the *Revised Standard Version Second Catholic Edition*. Most scriptures will be RSV2CE, unless otherwise noted to be the NAB. To use this book, you don't have to have any prior knowledge of scripture. You can be a beginner to the Bible who wants to memorize scripture, or you can have heard the Bible your whole life at Mass but want to have the "word of God dwell in you richly" (Col 3:16). Just remember—each scripture memorized is one more than you knew before! I hope this book and the Word of God within it inspires you and encourages you. Happy memorizing!

GETTING STARTED

Tips and Tricks for Memorizing Scripture

Memorization literally changes the brain and helps prevent cognitive decline. That means that committing scripture to memory can help you grow in many ways, no matter how young or old you are. It's important to begin this journey with the confidence that memorizing scripture is only going to help your brain and heart and soul for the better!

In addition to the tips below, you can join me on my weekly podcast, *Memorize Scripture*, which you can listen to on Spotify or Apple podcasts through avemariapress.com/memorize-scripture (or by using the QR code at right). It can be daunting to think about how many books I still haven't read or how much of scripture I haven't memorized. That's why I started the podcast, where I learn one scripture a week or four passages per month. That way, it's not overwhelming, and at the end of a month, I've already learned four scriptures. If you join me and stick with it for a year, you will have memorized forty-eight scriptures! Every week, you are not only gaining more knowledge of scripture, but you are also strengthening your brain.

Let's Memorize Scripture!

Here are some actionable tips and tricks to get you started:

- **Choose a Scripture Verse Each Week.** Select only one verse to learn each week. This manageable pace helps you stay on track, even if life gets busy and you miss a day or two.
- **Display the Verse Prominently.** Write the scripture where you'll frequently see it. Consider using your bathroom mirror, a sticky note in the kitchen, or a card in your car. You might also place it as a bookmark in your current read or anywhere else you'll see it regularly.
- **Copy the Verse.** Using the space provided in each chapter of this book, copy the verses you're trying to memorize. Copying is a great way to commit new content to memory

since it gets your body involved and requires you to commit the energy and time required by handwriting.

- **Recite It Daily.** Practice reciting the verse every day. You can write it out in a journal dedicated to your scripture verses or listen to a podcast that features daily recitations. The more you repeat it, the more familiar it will become.

- **Revisit Previous Verses.** As you add new scriptures, continue to review the ones you've already learned. My family and I print out our verses and place them in sheet protectors, organized on a key ring and hung on our wall. During our evening devotions, we recite all the verses to keep them fresh. You might also use note cards or another system that works for you.

- **Involve Others.** Memorizing with a partner, family member, or group can enhance motivation and accountability. Many find it helpful to learn along with their children, spouse, friends, or church community. When you gather, recite the scriptures together. For added fun, use an incentive to reward memorization, like the prize basket in my friend's church.

- **Try the Circle Game.** If memorizing with others, try the circle game where each person says the next word of the verse. My kids enjoy this game because it combines fun with a bit of friendly competition.

- **Be Creative.** Utilize your preferred learning style. If you're musically inclined, compose a song with the scripture. If you're artistic, create a visual piece featuring the verse. For those with a sense of humor, recite it in different voices. My kids like to add hand motions, which helps all of us remember the verses better.

Have fun, recite often, and happy memorizing!

ONE

God's Love

I love love stories. I love love songs. I remember, as a little girl, listening to the radio and hearing love songs. My young heart would rise with hope and desire as I sang along with Whitney Houston's "I Will Always Love You" or Celine Dion's "Because You Loved Me," and I dreamed that maybe someday I would have someone who loved me like that. When I heard sad songs about breakups or cheating or loss, my heart would fill with hurt and sadness at the thought that maybe love doesn't always work out or last forever. Songs like Adele's "Someone Like You," or Gotye's "Somebody That I Used to Know," and even Olivia Rodrigo's "Driver's License" became massive hits because they played such deep chords of sadness (and often familiarity) in our hearts, echoing that we were never meant to be abandoned, cheated on, betrayed, used, abused, or brokenhearted.

We know inherently what love is and what love isn't. Placed within the heart of every human being is a desire for an unconditional love that lasts forever. We know that love is not supposed to last for two hours, two weeks, two months, or two years, but for all eternity. We also know that love isn't abuse, use, betrayal, or abandonment.

How do we inherently know that? And why is the desire to love and to be loved so strong in all of our hearts—not just every Catholic heart, but every *human* heart?

Well, the *Catechism of the Catholic Church* states that "the desire for God is written in the human heart" because we were created by God and for God, who never stops drawing us to himself, and that for our whole lives we will search for truth and happiness that will be found "only in God" (27). God created us with these desires, and they are so good!

Genesis 1:27 says that we were created in the image and likeness of God, and 1 John 4:16 says, "God is love." It logically follows that because we were made in the image and likeness of our God who is love itself, stamped in our hearts is this desire to love and to be loved. As Mother Teresa of Calcutta pointed out, we weren't just made for business degrees or success or to be a number, but we were made for greater things—to love and to be loved. And every human being knows this on some level. We know that no amount of money, success, or popularity is ever enough to satisfy a heart that was created for God. No amount of followers or likes on social media will ever fill that hole in our heart that was meant for eternity. While we know in a general sense what love is and what love isn't, let's dive into a deeper understanding of God's love.

God's love is *diffusive*, which is a big word that just means it "goes out" and creates. Love can't be contained or kept in, just as when you fall in love, you have to go and tell the whole world! Thus, "God, infinitely perfect and blessed in himself, in a plan of sheer goodness freely created man to make him share in his own blessed life" (CCC, 1). We see this in the book of Genesis, when God creates the world. His love goes forth and creates the stars, the moon, and the sun, the flying things and the creepy-crawly things, the animals, and then us humans. Every day, God says his creation is "good." But after God creates humans, he says, "It is very good" (Gn 1:31). The *Catechism* explains, "All creatures bear a certain resemblance to God, most especially man, created in the image and likeness of God" (41).

"Most especially man." There is something special about being human. Because we are made in the image and likeness of God, we are made in the image and likeness of the Trinity. And the Trinity is not a solitude, but a communion of persons—Father, Son, and Holy Spirit. This gives a deeper meaning to the passage from Genesis where God says to Adam, "It is not good that the man should be alone" (2:18). We know deep in our hearts that we aren't meant to be alone, either. Anyone who has experienced a wound of abandonment feels or hears the lie that we are "all alone." The truth is that we are never alone! God is always with us, as it says in scripture: "Can a woman forget her sucking child, that she should have no compassion on the son of her womb? Even these may forget, yet I will not forget you" (Is 49:15), and Jesus says in Matthew 28:20, "Behold, I am with you always."

But God doesn't just desire to be with us or next to us—he desires to be *one* with us. That's the difference between a spouse saying, "I want to walk next to you for the rest of my life," and saying, "I want to be *one* with you for the rest of my life." How incredible that the God of the universe desires such intimacy and communion with us—and not just on earth, but for all eternity! The *Catechism* teaches that this is the great "secret" of our faith: "By sending his only Son and the Spirit of Love in the fullness of time, God has revealed his innermost secret: God himself is an eternal exchange of love, Father, Son and Holy Spirit, and he has destined us to share in that exchange" (CCC, 221).

God has destined us to be in communion with him for all eternity, in his "eternal exchange of love." We are invited to be one with him whose very being is love forever. And his love is not just a feeling—it is not fickle or fleeting—as our human love can be. His love is unconditional and sacrificial. God "proves his love for us in that while we were still sinners Christ died for us" (Rom 5:8, NAB). That means that God loves us no matter what. We can't earn his love, and we can't lose his love. He loves us just as much whether we act like sweet children of God or like little brats of God. He loves us just as much whether we are straight out of Confession and feel happy and free or have committed our worst sin and are filled with shame and guilt. Nothing "will be able to separate us from the love of God in Christ Jesus our Lord" (Rom 8:39, NAB).

The beautiful thing is, when we come to know how beloved we are by God, we respond to God not out of fear of hell but out of a desire to love him with our whole heart, mind, body, soul, and strength (Mk 12:30). Just as I don't do things for my husband out of fear that he will divorce me, but because I love him, we are meant to have a love for God that has no fear, and to do things for him out of love, not fear. The apostle John says it this way: "There is no fear in love, but perfect love casts out fear. For fear has to do with punishment, and he who fears is not perfected in love" (1 Jn 4:18). When we come to know God's powerful, unconditional love, it is life-changing. When we "know and believe the love God has for us" (1 Jn 4:16), we will naturally abide in God and let God abide in us.

This unconditional, sacrificial love (*agape* in Greek) is how we are called to love in this life. A scribe asked Jesus which of the 613 commandments in the Hebrew Bible (the Old Testament) was the most important. Jesus responded:

> The first is, "Hear O Israel: The Lord our God, the
> Lord is one; and you shall love the Lord your God
> with all your heart, and with all your soul, and
> with all your mind, and with all your strength."
> The second is this, "You shall love your neighbor
> as yourself." There is no other commandment
> greater than these.
>
> **MARK 12:29–31**

Knowing God's love for us enables us to love God, our-selves, and others in the proper way—not selfishly, but self-lessly, not based on feelings, but by *willing the good of the other.* It is only possible to love this way because "[God] first loved us" (1 Jn 4:19). I only know how to love my husband, my children, and my family and friends unconditionally because God first loved me unconditionally. The marriage vows reflect this type of commitment. We don't have "conditional" vows that say, "I will love you until you get old, fat, ugly, mean," and so on; we say, "I promise to love you in good times and in bad, in sickness and in health, 'til death do us part." That is a massively difficult thing to do, and it takes a lifetime to do it well. But that's the meaning of sacrifice—doing something whether you want to or not because of its inherent value. Jesus died for you and for me because we are inherently valuable to him: "Greater love has no man than this, that a man lay down his life for his friends" (Jn 15:13).

The God of the universe, our God who *is* love, laid down his life for us because he loves us so much. He wants us to spend eternity with him in heaven and be *one* with him.

God, thank you for your love. Thank you for the beauty of creation and for creating me in your image and likeness. You call me "very good," and you love me! You have created me out of love and by love and for love. Open my heart to receive your life-giving love. Show me places where I am apathetic toward you or fearful of your love. Pour out your graces of agape love into my heart, so I may experience the warmth of your love and share that love with others. Amen.

Ponder

* When you hear, "God loves you," what stirs in your heart?

✳ Do you feel like you have to earn God's love? Why or
   why not?

✳ Do you think God loves other people more than he loves
   you? Why or why not?

✳ What do you struggle with the most—loving God, loving
  your neighbor, or loving yourself?

Memorize

Choose one or more primary or secondary verses to work on
this week or this month. Head to "Let's Memorize Scripture!"
on page xxii to select a method to help you memorize your
choices.

One

We love,

because he first loved us.

1 JOHN 4:19

Two

But God

proves his love for us

in that while we were
still sinners

Christ died for us.

ROMANS 5:8 NAB

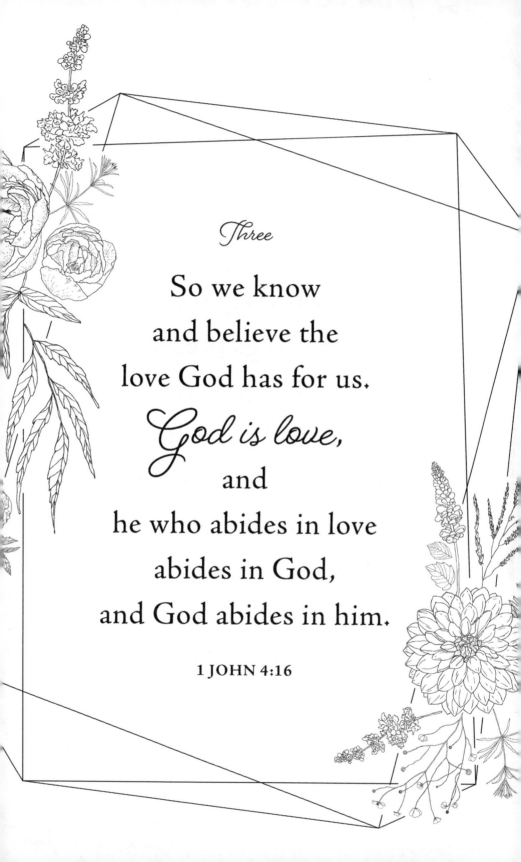

Three

So we know
and believe the
love God has for us.
God is love,
and
he who abides in love
abides in God,
and God abides in him.

1 JOHN 4:16

For I am sure that
neither death, nor life,
nor angels,
nor principalities,
nor things present,
nor things to come,
nor powers, nor height,
nor depth, nor anything
else in all creation,
will be able to separate us
from the love of God
in Christ Jesus
our Lord.

ROMANS 8:38–39

ALTERNATIVE VERSES

Five

For the mountains may depart and the hills be removed, but my mercy shall not depart from you, and my covenant of peace shall not be removed, says the LORD, who has compassion on you.

ISAIAH 54:10

Six

The steadfast love of the LORD never ceases, his mercies never come to an end; they are new every morning; great is your faithfulness.

LAMENTATIONS 3:22–23

Seven

I have loved you with an everlasting love; there-fore I have continued my faithfulness to you.

JEREMIAH 31:3b

Eight

Know therefore that the LORD your God is God,
the faithful God who keeps covenant and steadfast love with those who love him and keep his
commandments, to a thousand generations.

DEUTERONOMY 7:9

Nine

Greater love has no man than this, that a man
lay down his life for his friends.

JOHN 15:13

Ten

Your mercy, O LORD, extends to the heavens,
your faithfulness to the clouds.

PSALM 36:5

Write the weekly scripture on a sticky note and stick it on your bathroom mirror, or take a dry-erase marker and write the scripture verse on your bathroom mirror, so when you're getting ready every morning you see it. Use the space provided to practice copying your chosen verses. Write each verse at least three times.

TWO

The Good News

Years ago, I spoke to a group of about eighty Confirmation students (ages fifteen and sixteen) at a Catholic parish. After my talk, I asked if I could join in on one of their small groups where they discuss questions about the evening's topic with their adult leader. Because Confirmation is sometimes seen as a time when kids "graduate" from their faith and then leave the Church because they don't know or care about their faith and aren't forced to be there anymore, I wanted to see if these students understood why they were Catholic or even the basic Gospel message. So I asked the group of seven young ladies, "Can you tell me what the Good News is?" They looked at me with blank stares, almost as if I were speaking in a different language. Seeking to clarify the question, I said, "If there is Good News, that must mean there is bad news. What's the bad news?" Again, blank stares. Going further, I asked, "Why did Jesus die? Why was he crucified?" Finally, a young lady

timidly said, "For our sins?" "Yes!" I answered enthusiasti-
cally. I continued on to give them a very brief version of the
basic Gospel message, and it went something like this:

> God loves you and created you out of love and in
> his image and likeness to be in relationship with
> him. He created us to live forever with him. We
> were never meant to die! But when sin entered the
> world through Adam and Eve, death also entered
> the world. The bad news is that our sin condemns
> us to hell—"the wages of sin [result of sin] is death"
> (Rom 6:23)—but the Good News is that God sent his
> Son Jesus to take our sin upon his shoulders, to die
> the death that we were supposed to die (1 Jn 4:10),
> so that we might have eternal life. Jesus's death
> opened the gates of heaven for us! And he wants us
> to live forever with him in heaven. And every day,
> especially when we go to Mass, we say thank you
> to God for his sacrifice—that he laid down his life
> for us, to save us from our sin. And he invites each
> and every one of us into relationship with him—to
> know, love, and serve him—and to glorify him with
> our entire life.

While some of the young women in the small group
looked at me like I had four heads, others seemed encouraged
and filled with a new fervor. This is how it normally goes
wherever I try to summarize the Good News! But whether
or not the recipient of the Good News is actually receptive

doesn't deter me from sharing it. Mother Teresa of Calcutta said that God expects me to be faithful and not successful, and as someone who shares the Good News often, I take that saying to heart.

Parents are the first evangelists of God's love to their children, and the Catholic Church calls every family a "domestic church." I therefore try to very simply sum up the Good News often with my kids, especially before we go to Mass. Our little pep talk in the car before we enter church goes something like this:

> *Me:* "Why do we go to Mass?"
>
> *Kids:* "To say thank you!" (The word *Eucharist* means "thanksgiving.")
>
> *Me:* "Why do we say thank you?"
>
> *Kids:* "Because Jesus died on the Cross for us!"
>
> *Me:* "And why did he die on the Cross for us?"
>
> *Kids:* "To save us from our sins!"
>
> *Me:* "And why did he do that?"
>
> *Kids:* "Because he wants to spend eternity with us in heaven!"
>
> (And now that some of my kids are old enough to receive the Eucharist, they also know that we go to Mass to receive Jesus, body, blood, soul, and divinity, into our very bodies because he wants to be *that* close to us!)

The reason John 3:16 is one of the most quoted scripture verses in the world, and you see it displayed on billboards and painted under football players' eyes and printed on people's hats and shirts, is that it sums up the Gospel message so beautifully: "For God so loved the world that he gave his only-begotten Son, that whoever believes in him should not perish but have eternal life" (Jn 3:16).

The word *Gospel* means "good news," and it is such good news that even though the result of my sin is death, "The free gift of God is eternal life in Christ Jesus our Lord" (Rom 6:23). My sin does not define me, and your sin does not define you. Our sin and the condemnation that follows from it are *not* the end of our story! Scripture says that "for our sake he made him to be sin who knew no sin, so that in him we might become the righteousness of God" (2 Cor 5:21).

It is such good news that God gave his Son for us so that we might be blameless and pure and righteous and holy! The *Catechism* explains that "the Word became flesh to make us *'partakers of the divine nature'*: 'For this is why the Word became man, and the Son of God became the Son of man: so that man, by entering into communion with the Word and thus receiving divine sonship, might become a son of God'" (460).

How beautiful that God doesn't just save us and leave us! He saves us and then invites us to become part of his family through Baptism. In Baptism we become sons and daughters: "For you did not receive the spirit of slavery to fall back into fear, but you have received the spirit of sonship. When we cry, 'Abba! Father!' it is the Spirit himself bearing witness with our spirit that we are children of God" (Rom 8:15–16).

So what is our response to this Good News, this great sacrifice, this Divine Love? We are called to "repent, and be baptized" (Acts 2:38), believe in him (Jn 3:16), and love him with our whole heart, mind, soul, body, and strength (Mk 12:30).

One time I spoke at a women's retreat and shared my testimony and conversion story. A sixty-five-year-old woman asked me, "What does it mean to have a conversion?" I told her that it simply means surrendering everything to Jesus and saying, "Jesus, I trust in you. I trust you with everything—my relationships, my job, my finances, my family—everything!" Because Jesus held nothing back on the Cross—he gave everything—he asks for everything in return. Many people give Jesus only one hour a week, when they go to church. But can you imagine if that's what we did in marriage? If I gave my husband only one hour of my week to talk with him and be with him, that would be a pretty sad marriage; most people would say it wouldn't last very long. The marital relationship requires *constant* communication, which allows for deeper intimacy, spiritually, emotionally, and physically.

And guess what? Jesus is our divine bridegroom (see John 3:29; Matthew 9:15), and he desires intimacy with us not only for all eternity in heaven but right here on earth. On the Cross, Jesus proposes his divine love story to each one of us. He says with his very life, "I give you all of me! I lay down my life for you!" And he desires everything from us in return, essentially saying, "Will you give me all of you—every heartache, pain, blessing, gift, trial, consolation—not just 'til death do us part,' but for all eternity? Will you give me all of you, every day, to love you and honor you and cherish you, to have and to hold you for all eternity?" His proposal is unlike any other; the question is, Will we accept it?

The whole Bible is God's love story for his people. From beginning to end, the most frequent analogy of God's love is that of a bridegroom for his bride: "Behold, you are beautiful, my love, behold, you are beautiful! Your eyes are doves behind your veil. . . . You have ravished my heart, my sister, my bride, you have ravished my heart with a glance of your eyes" (Sg 4:1, 9), and "As the bridegroom rejoices over the bride, so shall your God rejoice over you" (Is 62:5).

Even when the bride is unfaithful (through sin), he desires her back: "I will espouse you for ever; I will espouse you in righteousness and in justice, in steadfast love, and in mercy. I espouse you to me in faithfulness" (Hos 2:19–20). And God desires for us, his bride, not only to be saved from our sin, but to have life abundantly (Jn 10:10) and to be cleansed (Baptism) and nourished (the Eucharist) (see Ephesians 5:25, 29) so that one day we will participate in the wedding feast of the Lamb in heaven:

"Hallelujah! For the Lord our God the Almighty
reigns.

> Let us rejoice and exult and give him the glory,
> for the marriage of the Lamb has come,
> and his Bride has made herself ready;
> it was granted her to be clothed with fine linen,

bright and pure"—
for the fine linen is the righteous deeds of the saints.

> And the angel said to me, "Write this: Blessed
are those who are invited to the marriage supper of
the Lamb." (Rv 19:6–9)

This love story—which is God's story for you and for me—
makes my heart leap! It is the best news I have ever heard.

Pray

Jesus, thank you for laying your life down on the Cross for me
and for taking my sin upon your shoulders—all because you
love me and desire to be with me for all eternity in heaven.
Thank you for inviting me into your family! Give me the graces to trust and surrender everything to you—all my fears, all
my weaknesses, my heartaches, my blessings, my vocation,
my time, my treasure, my talent, my family, my heart—all of
it to you! Jesus, my bridegroom, I am yours and you are mine.
Take all of me and use me for your glory!

Ponder

* When did you first hear the Good News?

* Have you ever shared the Good News with someone?

* What kind of relationship do you have with Jesus? Is
  it based on rules, or is it more of a bride/bridegroom
  relationship?

* Is there anything you are holding back from entering into full intimacy with Jesus, the bridegroom?

Memorize

Choose one or more primary or secondary verses to work on this week or this month. Head to "Let's Memorize Scripture!" on page xxii to select a method to help you memorize your choices.

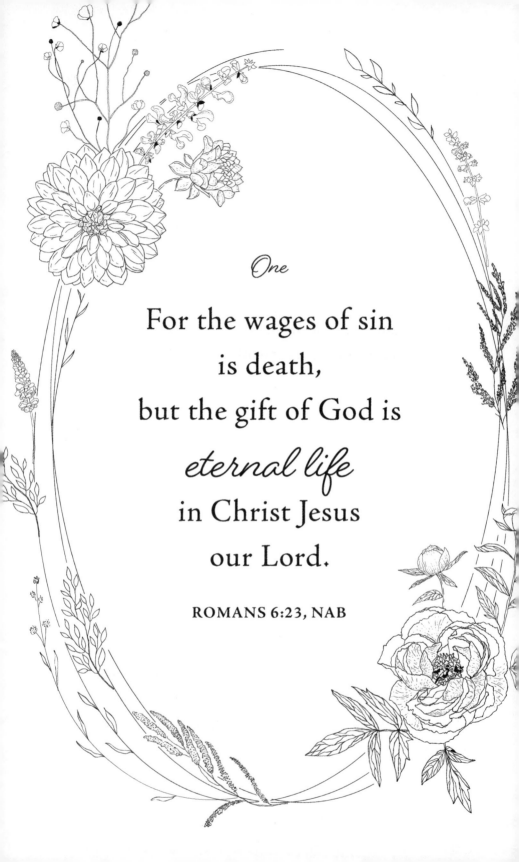

One

For the wages of sin
is death,
but the gift of God is

eternal life

in Christ Jesus
our Lord.

ROMANS 6:23, NAB

Two

For God
so loved the world
that he gave his only
Son, so that everyone
who believes in him
might not perish
but might have
eternal life.

JOHN 3:16, NAB

Three

The thief comes only
to steal and kill and
destroy; I came that they
may have life,
and have it abundantly.

JOHN 10:10

Four

Jesus said to him,
*"I am the way, and
the truth, and the life;*
no one comes to the
Father, but by me."

JOHN 14:6

ALTERNATIVE VERSES

Five

And there is salvation in no one else, for there is no other name under heaven given among men by which we must be saved.

ACTS 4:12

Six

But you are a chosen race, a royal priesthood, a holy nation, God's own people, that you may declare the wonderful deeds of him who called you out of darkness into his marvelous light.

1 PETER 2:9

Seven

For by grace you have been saved through faith; and this is not your own doing, it is the gift of God—not because of works, lest any man should boast.

EPHESIANS 2:8–9

Eight

For our sake he made him to be sin who knew
no sin, so that in him we might become the
righteousness of God.

2 CORINTHIANS 5:21

Nine

Now after John was arrested, Jesus came into
Galilee, preaching the gospel of God, and saying, "The time is fulfilled, and the kingdom
of God is at hand; repent, and believe in the
gospel."

MARK 1:14–15

Ten

He saved us, not because of deeds done by
us in righteousness, but in virtue of his own
mercy, by the washing of regeneration and
renewal in the Holy Spirit, which he poured out
upon us richly through Jesus Christ our Savior,
so that we might be justified by his grace and
become heirs in hope of eternal life.

TITUS 3:5–7

Practice

Pick a time of day to review your verse(s) that best fits your schedule, whether it's in the morning getting ready, or during a lunch break, or at bedtime prayer. Use the space provided to practice copying your chosen verses. Write each verse at least three times.

THREE

God Is Our Strength

If you or anyone you know has gone through the twelve-step program for recovering alcoholics, you may know that the first step of the program is to admit you have a problem—to admit that you don't have power over alcohol, but that alcohol has power over you and has made your life unmanageable. In the Christian life, we can use a very similar first step in the journey of becoming a disciple of Jesus Christ—admit that we have a problem called sin, and that we have not had power over sin, but that sin has had power over us and made our lives unmanageable. We must admit that we are not perfect and that we cannot save ourselves no matter how hard we try.

Our inclination to sin is called *concupiscence*. The desire to choose what feels good in the moment, rather than what is right or what is actually good, reveals that sin has power over us. It could be some form of the sin of pride, like having to always be right (arrogance), being fixated on our appearance (vanity), or speaking ill of others to try to prove we are better (gossip). It could be the sin of sloth, where we miss church on Sundays because sports or social commitments have taken precedence or where we forgo prayer because we are binge-watching a show or in an endless scroll on social media. It could be the sin of lust, where we can't stop our pornography habit, we keep crossing the boundaries of sexual intimacy with someone we aren't married to, or we allow ourselves to fantasize about that guy or gal who isn't our spouse. It could be the sin of anger, where our temper controls us and we can't control it when we're driving, getting into arguments, having to wait for things, or exploding when our kids do something kid-like. It could be the sin of greed, where we desire more possessions or wealth even if it means steamrolling or exploiting other people. It could be the sin of gluttony, where food or alcohol starts controlling us instead of our consuming it in healthy moderation. It could be the sin of envy, where we rejoice at someone's downfall or pain, or we seethe at someone's blessings or good fortune.

The Good News is that Jesus didn't come to save the perfect, or the sinless, or the strong. He came to save the messy, the sinners, the weak. Jesus makes this very clear in the gospels: "Those who are well have no need of a physician, but those who are sick; I came not to call the righteous, but sinners" (Mk 2:17). In the Sermon on the Mount, he flips everything on its head. Blessed aren't the rich, but the poor! Blessed aren't the powerful, but the meek! Blessed aren't the self-righteous, but those who "hunger and thirst for righteousness, for they shall be satisfied" (Mt 5:6). Blessed aren't the ones with fame and status, but those who are "persecuted for righteousness' sake, for theirs is the kingdom of heaven" (Mt 5:10).

That is such good news! So often, I feel like I have to be perfect to come before the Lord, or I have to be the strong one, holding it all together. Those of us who struggle with control have a hard time delegating, even if it is to the Lord, because we fear looking weak or incompetent, or because we have a wound where we feel that people haven't come through for us. Yet the reality is that "when I am weak, then I am strong" (2 Cor 12:9–10). I do not have to rely on myself (called "unholy self-reliance") for everything, because apart from God, I can do nothing (Jn 15:5). All my strength comes from the Lord, and with him, I can do all things (Phil 4:13).

This is the beauty of conversion. For so long, we have controlled every aspect of our lives—from financial decisions to family to jobs—not realizing that it was really pride that controlled us. It is pride that says, "I can do better than God" or "I know better than God." And underneath that sentiment is really a fear that maybe God won't provide or maybe God is holding out on me. Maybe God loves other people more, because he gives other people good things, but not me. But conversion is surrendering it all. It is saying, "God, I *need* you. I can't do this on my own. I can't save myself! I am weak, but *you* are strong! I need your strength. You are my rock, my fortress, my refuge. Wrap me in your arms. Wrap me in your love." Psalm 18 sums it up beautifully: "I love you, O Lord, my strength" (NAB).

A conversion is like a hardened heart melting or a flower unfolding. You've probably sung the hymn "Joyful, Joyful, We Adore Thee" at Mass. There's a line that says, "Hearts unfold like flowers before thee, opening to the sun above"; that's what happens when we experience a conversion. We become vulnerable (maybe for the first time), and we allow the Lord into places of our heart that no one else has seen or been. Many of us put up a strong facade but are really terrified of letting people into our lives for fear that we will be rejected or hurt. We think that if others truly knew us, they wouldn't love us or be friends with us anymore. But that is not how the Lord works. The Lord created us and knows every hair on our head and every desire of our heart. He has seen us in our most glorious moments and our most shameful moments, and he still loves us! He loves being the Father who holds us in his arms when we are dejected or hurt, and he loves lavishing us with gifts when we ask him to provide. C. S. Lewis puts it this way:

To love at all is to be vulnerable. Love anything and
your heart will be wrung and possibly broken. If
you want to make sure of keeping it intact you must
give it to no one, not even an animal. Wrap it care-
fully round with hobbies and little luxuries; avoid
all entanglements. Lock it up safe in the casket or
coffin of your selfishness. But in that casket, safe,
dark, motionless, airless, it will change. It will not
be broken; it will become unbreakable, impenetra-
ble, irredeemable. To love is to be vulnerable. (*The
Four Loves*)

In my own life, before my conversion, God was just a
convenience, and church was something I did because my
mom made me go. I didn't really *need* God (or so I thought),
because I was accomplishing enough on my own. But when
God gently touched my heart during adoration when I was
eighteen years old, I recognized that my whole life was about
glorifying myself. I realized that I had wounds of rejection
and fear that propelled me to be a people pleaser, and I longed
for affirmation from people (whether boyfriends or friends or
teachers) because I didn't have that security in Christ. Jesus
infused me with a dose of humility, allowing me to see that
while I was projecting the image of a strong, have-it-all-to-
gether, confident gal, my desires were actually warped, as I
sought my worth in unholy relationships and achievements,
instead of in God alone.

For the first time in my life I realized that being vulnerable and admitting my failures was not a weakness, but a strength. For the first time, my unholy self-reliance was transformed into reliance on God. I felt so strong with him in me and by my side! And I felt unstoppable. When I went to college and experienced persecution and mockery for my Catholic faith, it emboldened me as St. Paul said: "Therefore, I am content with weaknesses, insults, hardships, persecutions, and constraints, for the sake of Christ; for when I am weak, then I am strong" (2 Cor 12:10, NAB). Later, when I was traveling constantly, battling exhaustion and migraines and throwing up in airplane bags as a result, I learned to bask in his call to "Come to me all you who labor and are burdened and I will give you rest" (Mt 11:28, NAB). And when I've experienced suffering with health issues—when I was hospitalized twice in two months for a post-miscarriage hemorrhage and a rare kidney abscess and then experienced another two miscarriages soon after—I've thrown myself into God's arms, feeling powerless, hopeless, confused, and exhausted, but praying constantly, "Jesus, I trust in you," and feeling very tangibly that God was my "refuge and strength, a very present help in trouble" (Ps 46:1).

It is so beautiful when you can finally relax, rest, take refuge in, and rely on the Lord. It is so relieving when you realize you don't have to have it all together, you don't have to look perfect or project the "perfect life" to others. On the contrary, others around you will be grateful and inspired by your willingness to be human, to show your weaknesses and struggles and vulnerabilities. In turn, those people around you will also allow themselves to be vulnerable in response to your witness. And do you know what can happen when the "heart unfolds like flowers"? It releases the most beautiful fragrance. I'm not just speaking metaphorically here. One of the miraculous signs of holiness can be a sweet fragrance. Some people report that they have smelled roses when Mother Mary is present, and some saints (such as Mother Teresa of Calcutta) have had the "fragrance of Christ" and smelled like roses when they walked by.

I know that, like a delicate flower, you might be afraid to be crushed when you unfold in vulnerability before another. It is what happened to Jesus on the Cross. He was crushed for our sake and for our sins. But guess what? He did that so that he might be our strength when we are crushed. He did that so you wouldn't have to rely on yourself anymore or pretend to be strong when your heart is broken in a million pieces. Come to him, and he will give you rest. He will be your strength and give you strength.

Pray

Jesus, come into the mess of my heart. You know my weaknesses and my warped desires and yet you still love me. Lord, come into the places where I desire other things more than you and the places where I am afraid to let go of control. Lord, I need you, for I am weak, yet you are strong. I need you to be my shelter and strength when I am in trouble, when I am lost, when I am afraid. Help me to be vulnerable with you and with others when all I want to do sometimes is run or hide or deflect. God, you are gentle with my heart, and I trust in you.

Ponder

* What are you afraid of when you think of being vulnerable?

✳ Who is the easiest person in your life to be vulnerable
   with?

✳ What time in your life were you the most weak? Who or
   what did you turn to? Did you turn to God, or did you
   turn to something else to pacify the pain?

Memorize

Choose one or more primary or secondary verses to work on
this week or this month. Head to "Let's Memorize Scripture!"
on page xxii to select a method to help you memorize your
choices.

One

God is our refuge
and strength, a very
present help in trouble.

PSALM 46:1

Two

I can do all things
in him
who strengthens me.

PHILIPPIANS 4:13

Three

Come to me,
all you who labor
and are burdened, and
I will give you rest.
Take my yoke upon you
and learn from me, for I
am meek and humble of
heart; and you will find
rest for yourselves.
For my yoke is easy,
and my burden
light.

MATTHEW 11:28–30, NAB

But he said to me,

"*My grace is sufficient* for you, for power is made perfect in weakness." I will rather boast most gladly of my weaknesses, in order that the power of Christ may dwell with me. Therefore, I am content with weaknesses, insults, hardships, persecutions, and constraints, for the sake of Christ; for when I am weak, then I am strong.

2 CORINTHIANS 12:9–10, NAB

ALTERNATIVE VERSES

Five

Fear not, for I am with you,
    be not dismayed, for I am your God;
I will strengthen you, I will help you,
    I will uphold you with my victorious right
    hand.

ISAIAH 41:10

Six

The LORD is my strength and my shield;
    in him my heart trusts;
so I am helped, and my heart exults,
    and with my song I give thanks to him.

PSALM 28:7

Seven

Have I not commanded you? Be strong and of
good courage; be not frightened, neither be
dismayed; for the LORD your God is with you
    wherever you go.

JOSHUA 1:9

Eight

He who dwells in the shelter of the Most High,
who abides in the shadow of the
Almighty, will say to the LORD, "My refuge
and my fortress;
my God, in whom I trust."
For he will deliver you from the snare of
the fowler
and from the deadly pestilence;
he will cover you with his pinions,
and under his wings you will find refuge;
his faithfulness is a shield and buckler.

PSALM 91:1–4

Nine

And do not be grieved, for the joy of the LORD
is your strength.

NEHEMIAH 8:10b

Ten

On the day I called, you answered me,
my strength of soul you increased.

PSALM 138:3

Practice

Take your scripture to prayer, whether it's in the presence of the Blessed Sacrament or some other quiet space. Repeat it over and over and let his word dwell in you and speak to you as you pray. Use the space provided to journal during your prayer time. Also, practice copying your chosen verses. Write each verse at least three times.

FOUR

Rejoice!

In 2005, the television show *60 Minutes* interviewed quarterback Tom Brady, who at that point had won three Super Bowls (he has now won seven). He was married to an actress and model (the first of two), had a multimillion-dollar NFL contract, and had reached what appeared to be the pinnacle of a happy, fulfilled life: fame, money, good looks, romance, power, position, celebrity status, and so forth.

One part of the interview went like this:

> *Tom Brady:* "Why do I have three Super Bowl rings and still think there's something greater out there for me? I mean, maybe a lot of people would say, 'Hey man, this is what it is. I've reached my goal, my life. . . .' Me, I think, 'God, there's gotta be more than this. This can't be what's it all cracked up to be.'"

Interviewer: "What's the answer?"
Tom Brady: "I wish I knew, I wish I knew."

My mouth dropped open as I watched the interview, and I yelled at the screen, "It's Jesus! The answer is Jesus!" Come to find out, Tom Brady was baptized Catholic at a church in Boston (I spoke there once, and they were very proud of the fact!). And yet, no one ever told him, "Hey man, you can have all the money in the world, all the fame in the world, all the supermodels in the world, and there will still be something missing in your life if you don't have God!"

That ache in our heart for "something more" isn't new. As long as humans have existed, that ache has existed. Why? Because God put it there! St. Augustine said, "You have made us for yourself, O Lord, and our heart is restless until it rests in you." He recognized this ache back in the early 400s. Over the centuries before and since, people have been trying to satisfy the ache of their hearts for "something more" with power, money, honor, and/or pleasure. It never works!

Tom Brady admitted that reaching the top was not enough to satisfy his heart. Money and fame don't satisfy a heart that was made for "something more." In *Mere Christianity*, C. S. Lewis wrote that every earthly desire we have can be satisfied—hunger with food, thirst with drink, sexual desire with sex. But there is a desire for "something more" that nothing on earth can satisfy, suggesting that there must be a "something more" that *does* exist. Lewis says, "If I find in myself a desire which no experience in this world can satisfy, the most probable explanation is that I was made for another world."

As Catholics, we know that "something more" is eternity—specifically, an eternity with God, who is love, in heaven. In heaven we will experience "this perfect life with the Most Holy Trinity—this communion of life and love with the Trinity, with the Virgin Mary, the angels and all the blessed" (*CCC*, 1024). The *Catechism* says beautifully that "heaven is the ultimate end and fulfillment of the deepest human longings, the state of supreme, definitive happiness" (1024).

Since heaven is our ultimate destiny and happiness, the experience of being here on earth will always feel like the journey of a pilgrim, who is traveling toward the goal of "citizenship . . . in heaven" (Phil 3:20, NAB). Even while having a life in Christ here on earth and knowing a "peace that surpasses all understanding" (Phil 4:7, NAB), we will still have an ache in our heart for our true home, which is heaven. For me, that is extremely good reason to *rejoice*. My home is not here on earth, but in heaven, where there is no more "mourning nor crying nor pain . . . for the former things have passed away" (Rv 21:4).

Since I was little, I have thought about death and heaven. I was living *memento mori* (which means "remember your death" in Latin) before it was popular! This is all because my mother would often say to me during our bedtime prayers, "If God calls you home, remember one word: 'negotiate!'"

We would say the usual prayers (Our Father, Hail Mary, Guardian Angel prayer), and then we'd say that weirdly scary prayer, "Now I lay me down to sleep, I pray the Lord my soul to keep, if I should die before I wake . . ." and I remember thinking, "I'm five! I'm going to die!" I'm not totally off-base here, by the way. Not long ago, a horror movie called *My Soul to Keep* was released, and it just confirmed what I knew to be true: that little nighttime prayer was indeed scary! But what this led me to as a child was a constant remembrance that life is short, you don't know when your death is coming, and you aren't guaranteed eighty or ninety years. And the church fathers' phrase *memento mori* was not meant to be scary but encouraging, because if you remember that one day you are going to die, you will focus on how to actually *live*. Or, as the cinematic prophet William Wallace says in *Braveheart*, "Every man dies. Not every man really lives."

Thankfully, after my conversion, death didn't seem so scary. I read St. Paul's writings where he expressed his longing to die to be with God in heaven, knowing that he was still on earth because God was using him to build up the kingdom. He wrote to the Philippians: "For to me to live is Christ, and to die is gain. . . . My desire is to depart and be with Christ, for that is far better. But to remain in the flesh is more necessary on your account. Convinced of this, I know that I shall remain and continue with you all, for your progress and joy in the faith" (1:21, 23b–25). I felt the same way. I couldn't wait to be in heaven with Jesus! For all of us humans who have experienced hurt and sickness and suffering here on earth, the thought of heaven—of paradise—gives so much hope.

When our goal is heaven, our perspective changes. *Perspective* comes from the Latin verb *perspicere* (*per-* "through" + *specere* "to look"), which literally means "to look through." When you're a Christian who believes in eternal life in heaven, your perspective allows you to "look through" every tough situation on earth because your hope is in heaven where there is no more weeping or suffering or pain or sadness. We can rejoice always in every circumstance, because we were not made for this world, and even death has no sting, no power over us (1 Cor 15:55). So I rejoice that even though I have lost faithful loved ones here on earth, I will see them in heaven someday. I rejoice that all my physical ailments (and even *your* physical ailments) will be transformed and made new in heaven. I rejoice that even if I am mocked for my faith here on earth, an entire community of saints waits to welcome me in heaven, many of whom have been tested and tried and have suffered much more than I have.

I think of St. José Luis Sánchez del Río, a fourteen-year-old martyr during the Cristero War in the 1920s. The Mexican government persecuted Catholics, even to the point of death. St. José was part of the resistance and was captured during a battle and imprisoned. But José's faith was not shaken. He saw a fellow prisoner being tortured and encouraged him, saying, "You will be [in] heaven before me. Prepare a place for me. Tell Christ the King I shall be with him soon." The soldiers cut the bottoms of St. José's feet and made him march through town to his own grave. They kept tempting him to renounce his faith, urging him to say, "Death to Christ the King!" in order to spare his life. But José would not relent. He prayed the Rosary and shouted, "Viva Cristo Rey!" (Long live Christ the King!). When they got to the place where they had dug his grave, the soldiers gave him another chance to renounce his faith. But José shouted again, "Viva Cristo Rey!" and they shot him to death.

José's death (and every other martyr's death) would seem purposeless if we didn't believe in heaven. But because we do believe in heaven, St. José's death is inspiring and convicting and drives me to want to live a life worthy of the call of heaven, whether I die safely in my bed or at the weapon of choice of an enemy of Christianity. May we always rejoice that this world is not our home—that we have a home in heaven, and it is paradise!

Pray

Jesus, I can't wait to be with you in heaven! Help me to live this journey of life well, running the race toward heaven with the help of your grace and all the angels and saints cheering me on! Help me to remember that life is not about money, power, pleasure, or honor, but it is about glorifying you and loving and serving you with all my heart, mind, body, and soul. Lord, give me perspective to see through the challenges of life and remember that I was made for an eternity of joy where there is no more weeping, suffering, sadness, or pain. Pour out your Holy Spirit upon me to give me courage, especially when it comes to suffering for you or being persecuted or mocked for your sake. St. José Luis Sánchez del Río, pray for me!

*   Apart from God, what are the things you rejoice in? What makes you happy?

* If you are looking for "something more," what do you
   think will make you happy? Is it more money? A different
   job? A different romantic partner? Something else?

* Do you struggle with hopelessness or feeling like things
   will never change?

* Do you have a fear of death? What are you most afraid about it?

Memorize

Choose one or more primary or secondary verses to work on this week or this month. Head to "Let's Memorize Scripture!" on page xxii to select a method to help you memorize your choices.

One

This is the day
which the LORD
has made; let us rejoice
and be glad in it!

PSALM 118:24

Two

Rejoice in the Lord always.
I shall say it again: rejoice!
Your kindness should be
known to all.

The Lord is near.

PHILIPPIANS 4:4–5, NAB

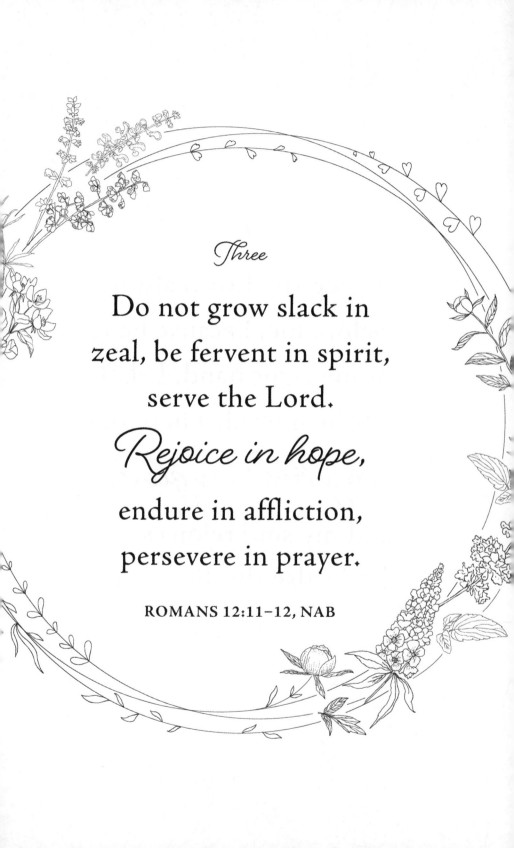

Three

Do not grow slack in zeal, be fervent in spirit, serve the Lord.

Rejoice in hope,

endure in affliction, persevere in prayer.

ROMANS 12:11–12, NAB

Four

I keep the Lord always before me; because he is at my right hand, I shall not be moved. Therefore *my heart is glad,* and my soul rejoices; my body also dwells secure.

PSALM 16:8–9

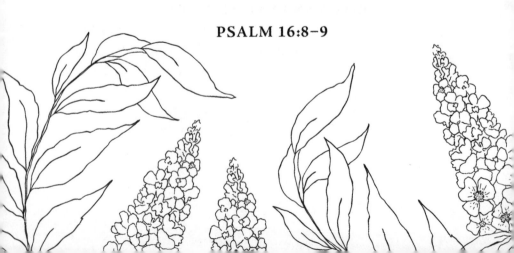

ALTERNATIVE VERSES

Five

Sing aloud, O daughter of Zion;
  shout, O Israel!
Rejoice and exult with all your heart,
  O daughter of Jerusalem! . . .
The LORD your God is in your midst,
  a warrior who gives victory;
he will rejoice over you with gladness,
  he will renew you in his love;
he will exult over you with loud singing.

ZEPHANIAH 3:14, 17

Six

Nevertheless do not rejoice in this, that the
spirits are subject to you; but rejoice that your
  names are written in heaven.

LUKE 10:20

Seven

But I have trusted in thy steadfast love;
   my heart shall rejoice in thy salvation.
I will sing to the LORD,
      because he has dealt bountifully with me.

PSALM 13:5–6

Eight

Without having seen him you love him; though
you do not now see him you believe in him and
rejoice with unutterable and exalted joy. As the
outcome of your faith you obtain the salvation
of your souls.

1 PETER 1:8–9

Nine

I will greatly rejoice in the LORD,
   my soul shall exult in my God;
for he has clothed me with the garments of
      salvation,
      he has covered me with the robe of
      righteousness,
as a bridegroom decks himself with a garland,
   and as a bride adorns herself with her jewels.

ISAIAH 61:10

Ten

The precepts of the LORD are right,
rejoicing the heart;
the commandment of the LORD is pure,
enlightening the eyes.

PSALM 19:8

Write down the first letter of each word of the scripture verse on a piece of paper or on a note card to jog your memory. For instance, "This is the day which the LORD has made; let us rejoice and be glad in it!" would be "T I T D W T L H M; L U R A B G I I." You can also use the space below for this exercise, or you can simply practice copying your chosen verses. Write each verse at least three times.

FIVE

Wonderfully Made

Growing up in the nineties, I was surrounded by images of anorexic models, belly-baring pop stars, and movies that denigrated the human body and sex (think *American Pie*), all without healthy navigation on these topics in my own personal upbringing. I had friends that struggled with anorexia or bulimia or cutting. As for me, I believed I wasn't good enough because my already hippy, size-6 frame at the age of fourteen was termed "plus-sized" by a modeling group for whom anything over a size 4 was "too big." On top of that, going through puberty and having acne featured prominently in school pictures and homecoming photos didn't help my self-esteem. While I was a pretty confident, outgoing teen, I still felt absolutely inadequate in my body—too tall, too fat, too much acne, too much cellulite, too much boobage, too many spider veins, and so on.

I'm sure none of you reading this can relate, right? Actually, you're probably reeling with the thoughts about your body that plagued you as a teen—whether they were instilled by pop culture or by your own mother or father. Perhaps your loved ones would regularly dote on or criticize your appearance, focusing on your too frizzy or too stick-straight hair, an oversized or misshaped nose, crooked or gapped teeth, a chin that stuck out or stayed in, boobs too big or too small, a body that looked "too big" or "too scrawny"—the list could go on and on.

Or maybe you intensely hated your body because an unwanted sexual encounter or abuse occurred at a young age, and you felt disgusted or ashamed by your body and how it felt and how it looked. These experiences stay with us our whole lives, oftentimes affecting our internal dialogue about ourselves and our dignity and worth, which, in turn, affects our relationships with God and others.

The place in our heart where there is shame, pain, disgust, or self-hatred regarding our body is also where Jesus—in his tenderness—meets us, receives us, and wraps us in his gentle love. Jesus did that with the woman at the well (see John 4)—the woman who had had five husbands and was living with another man who was not her husband—when he invited her to drink of the living water of new life he offered instead

of the stagnant water of shame and guilt. Jesus did that with
the woman caught in adultery in John 8; when all the other
religious leaders called her by her sin, he called her to "go
and sin no more." If Jesus treated those women with kindness
and respect, why do you think he won't do the same with
you? If you let him, he will look you in the eyes with love
and compassion and tenderness and tell you that you are not
your feelings of self-hatred, you are not your regrets or fears,
you are not your shame or pain, but you are his beautiful
beloved one, whom he longs to be with for all eternity. He
delights in you as the lover in the Song of Solomon delights
in his love: "Behold you are beautiful, my love!" (4:1). As St.
Catherine of Siena marveled, "What made you establish man
in so great a dignity? Certainly the incalculable love by which
you have looked on your creature in yourself! You are taken
with love for her; for by love indeed you created her, by love
you have given her a being capable of tasting your eternal
Good" (quoted in *CCC*, 356).

I am convinced that the devil is hell-bent on making us
hate our bodies and the bodies of others. The devil prowls
about seeking souls to devour (1 Pt 5:8), and I believe the
easiest way for him to hurt souls is through the desecration of
the body. This is so easily seen with the porn industry, which
profits off the exploitation of the human body (especially in
the sexual act) and makes more money than the NFL, MLB,
and NBA combined (https://www.defendyoungminds.com/

post/you-wont-believe-who-profits-from-porn). Doesn't it make sense that if your "body is a temple of the Holy Spirit" (1 Cor 6:19–20), then the devil would want to destroy that temple any way he can?

In his book *Love and Responsibility* (1960), St. John Paul II (then Cardinal Karol Wojtyla) predicted that in the future, the opposite of love wouldn't be hate; it would be *use*. That we would use people as objects instead of loving them as persons. But we aren't meant to use and be used; we are meant to love and be loved! And our bodies aren't meant for exploitation; they are meant to be reverenced. We are so blessed to have the writings of St. John Paul II, especially *Man and Woman He Created Them: A Theology of the Body*, which he delivered over the course of five years in his Wednesday papal audiences from 1979 to 1984. His teachings on the human person, marriage, and sex radically changed my views on identity, relationships, chastity, and marital love as I became familiar with his writings in my early twenties. I even met my husband at the Theology of the Body Institute in Pennsylvania, where we took a thirty-hour semester course on the theology of the body over a period of five days.

Here's a short version: In combating the heresies of Dualism and Manichaeism (which say "body bad and soul good") and in light of the sexual revolution, John Paul II wanted us to know that our bodies are not just biological, they are theological; they reveal something about God. Looking back at

Genesis, before sin entered the world, we can see that human beings were made male and female in the image and likeness of God, who is love (and as I mentioned in chapter 1, made in the image of the Trinity—a communion of Persons). We even see as male and female that our bodies don't make sense on their own, are incomplete on their own—that we are made for union and communion with the other, ultimately in marriage, where we become *one* flesh. This first marriage of Adam and Eve in Genesis is a foreshadowing of the last book of the Bible—Revelation—where we, the Church, the bride, become *one* with Jesus, the bridegroom. The ecstasies and joys of marital love are a foreshadowing of the ecstasies and joys of heaven.

In other words, our body isn't just a shell or prison where our soul resides. On the contrary, "The unity of soul and body is so profound that one has to consider the soul to be the 'form' of the body . . . spirit and matter, in man, are not two natures united, but rather their union forms a single nature" (*CCC*, 365). We are neither angels, who are rational spirits without bodies, nor animals, which are nonrational, bodily beings. We are human beings who have both a body and a rational soul. We can choose to love or to reject love. We can choose to reverence our bodies and others' bodies, or we can exploit, desecrate, use, or abuse them. Animals don't do that. That's why some people love animals more than humans. If we have been wounded by humans who have free will to choose good or evil, we feel safer with an animal that might hurt us because of instinct, but not because of a free, rational choice.

As humans, we are called to self-giving, unconditional love. Jesus appeals to our hearts by saying, "Every one who looks at a woman lustfully has already committed adultery with her in his heart" (Mt 5:28). We were not designed for lust (which is to use another as an object for pleasure); we were designed for God's *agape* love—sacrificial, unconditional, and a total gift of self. In *Gaudium et Spes*, John Paul II states, "Man is the only creature on earth which God willed for itself, [and he] cannot fully find himself except through a sincere gift of himself" (24). We are called to be gifts! Whether we are single, celibate, or married, we are all called to be gifts, to love and serve others as Jesus did. This great call to love reflects Jesus's love on the Cross, a love that is free, total, faithful, and fruitful. This is seen so profoundly in marriage, as a man and a woman make these four promises to each other (to love freely, totally, faithfully, fruitfully).

Love has to have these four pillars, or else it ceases to be love. Love has to be free—it can't be forced. Love has to be total—loving the whole person, not just loving part of them or what I can "get" from them (i.e., physical or emotional pleasure). Love has to be faithful—it forsakes all others and does not cheat or abandon. And love is fruitful—it is open to life; it is not contracepted spiritually or physically. A couple makes these promises with words on their wedding day, and then when they become *one* flesh during sex, those vows become flesh! So every time a married couple has sex, they are renewing their wedding vows! St. John Paul II calls these four marks of love the "language of the body." The body speaks a truth. That's why sex outside of marriage is a body that is telling something other than the truth, since the body is making a promise in sex ("I promise to love you freely, totally, faithfully, fruitfully") that it never actually made with words.

Our bodies are temples of the Holy Spirit (1 Cor 6:19–20). We are called to offer our bodies as a constant gift of love, to offer our bodies "as a living sacrifice" (Rom 12:1) as Jesus did. Our bodies are sacred. Sex is sacred.

Pray

Lord, thank you for creating my body good and holy and sacred, a glorious temple of your Holy Spirit! Help me to see my body and the bodies of others how you see them—to be reverenced and loved. In your name, Jesus, we ask for you to remove all shame and fear that surrounds our bodies and to replace it with your love and goodness and tenderness. Please forgive me for the times I have used another person as an object or for the times I have let another use me. Give me the grace of purity of heart, mind, body, and soul. Purify my memories and my imagination and help me to offer my body as a "living sacrifice" as you did on the Cross, so my life may be a gift to all I encounter.

* When was the first time you heard that your body was good or holy?

* What thoughts have you had about your body or appearance from your childhood to now?

✳ Have you ever used someone's body or allowed them to use you?

✳ How is God calling you to be a "gift of self" in your state of life? How can you love freely, totally, faithfully, and fruitfully as Jesus loved?

Memorize

Choose one or more primary or secondary verses to work on this week or this month. Head to "Let's Memorize Scripture!" on page xxii to select a method to help you memorize your choices.

One

You formed my inmost being; you knit me in my mother's womb. I praise you, so wonderfully you made me; wonderful are your works!

My very self you knew.

PSALM 139:13–14, NAB

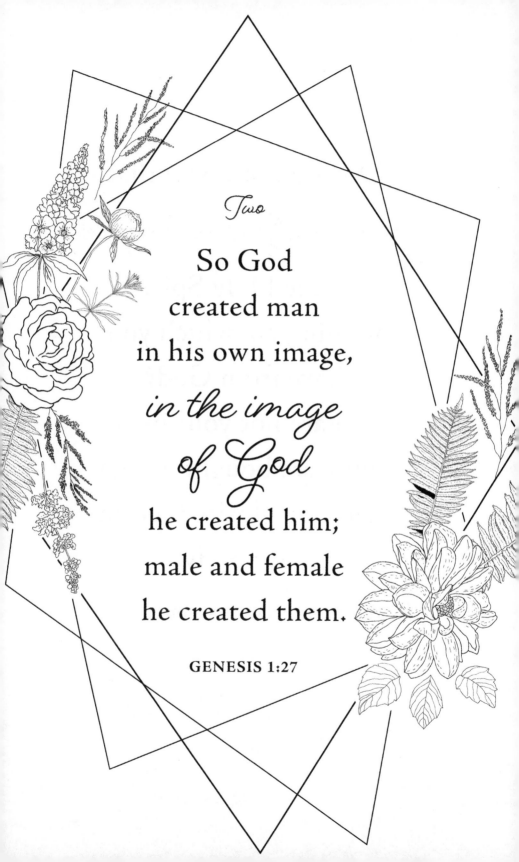

Two

So God
created man
in his own image,
in the image
of God
he created him;
male and female
he created them.

GENESIS 1:27

Three

Do you not know that

your body is a temple

of the Holy Spirit within you, which you have from God?

You are not your own; you were bought with a price. So glorify God in your body.

1 CORINTHIANS 6:19–20

Four

I urge you therefore,
brothers, by the mercies of
God, to offer your bodies as
a living sacrifice, holy and
pleasing to God, your spiritual
worship. Do not be conformed
to this world but be

*transformed by the
renewal of your mind,*

that you may prove what is the
will of God, what is good and
acceptable and perfect.

ROMANS 12:1–2, NAB

ALTERNATIVE VERSES

Five

May the God of peace himself sanctify you
wholly; and may your spirit and soul and body
be kept sound and blameless at the coming of
our Lord Jesus Christ.

1 THESSALONIANS 5:23

Six

Charm is deceitful, and beauty is vain,
But a woman who fears the Lord is to be
praised.

PROVERBS 31:30

Seven

Let not yours be the outward adorning with
braiding of hair, decoration of gold, and wear-
ing of robes, but let it be the hidden person
of the heart with the imperishable jewel of a
gentle and quiet spirit, which in God's sight is
very precious.

1 PETER 3:3-4

Eight

But the LORD said to Samuel, "Do not look on his appearance or on the height of his stature, because I have rejected him; for the LORD sees not as man sees; man looks on the outward appearance, but the LORD looks on the heart."

1 SAMUEL 16:7

Nine

For we are his workmanship, created in Christ Jesus for good works, which God prepared beforehand, that we should walk in them.

EPHESIANS 2:10

Ten

But our commonwealth is in heaven, and from it we await a Savior, the Lord Jesus Christ, who will change our lowly body to be like his glorious body, by the power which enables him even to subject all things to himself.

PHILIPPIANS 3:20–21

Practice

Be a gift to another by writing encouraging scriptures for your friends or family! This will not only be an act of kindness, but it will help you practice your memory verses! Write a little note, letter, text, or email of a scripture to ten of your friends, family members, fellow parishioners, or even acquaintances at work, the grocery store, or in your neighborhood. Use the space provided to practice copying your chosen verses. Write each verse at least three times.

SIX

Made New in Christ

I love witnessing transformation, whether it's watching our ugly, stick-like winter garden come alive in spring, with an explosion of purple salvias and hot pink roses and yellow daisies, or seeing our dilapidated 1960s-era bathroom turn into an inviting, spa-like oasis in a recent remodel. Transformations like these allow us to delight in the beauty and order of the renewed space, whether inside or outside. I could say the same thing about the human soul as well.

One of my favorite stories of all time is *A Christmas Carol*, by Charles Dickens. I have read the book; watched my husband's favorite movie version, *The Muppet Christmas Carol*, multiple times every year with our kids; and performed on stage more than once as Scrooge's young fiancée in Alan Menken's musical version. And even though I have gone through this story hundreds of times, I am still moved (often to tears) by the conversion of Ebenezer Scrooge. This man, who is prideful, selfish, greedy, and mean, sees the past and mourns his decisions—especially losing the love of his life—because they have left him alone and miserable. His misery, in turn, affects the people around him, from his employees to his neighbors to his nephew. As he flies from the past to the present to the future, he realizes that the man he has become in pursuit of money is one of the most hated and disregarded men in London, that he is inadvertently causing the death of his employee's son (Tiny Tim), and that he will one day be nothing more than a plot of earth for the worms to eat. This epiphany has jolted him, and the scales finally fall from his eyes, allowing him to realize that there is more to the meaning of life than wealth. He understands that being a gift to others will bring exponentially more value to his life than any amount of money ever could. To me, there is nothing more beautiful than this kind of realization and transformation. Nothing more beautiful than a heart that was once stony and cold becoming a heart of flesh, a heart of compassion, a heart that has repented of its old ways—a heart of beauty.

Every great story has a conversion or transformation of some sort, whether it's the harsh prejudgment that turns into love between Elizabeth Bennett and Mr. Darcy in *Pride and Prejudice*; or the selfishness of millionaire playboy Tony Stark in *Iron Man* that turns into a fatherly sacrificial gift even to death in *Avengers: Endgame*; or the fear, avoidance, and cowardice of Simba in *Lion King* that turn into strength and courage as he learns his identity and the truth of his past. And the greatest story ever told was that the God of the universe became man in Jesus Christ and laid down his life for us, so that we who were dead in our sins might be made new and have eternal life—that we who were once slaves to sin might be free. When the scales fall from our eyes and we accept Jesus into our hearts and lives, we become a "new creation," and the old has passed away and new things have come (2 Cor 5:17).

The gospels mention many who encountered Christ and became "new creations" (some named and some unnamed), but one of the most striking and impactful conversions in all of history was that of Saul, who became St. Paul. Because St. Paul's conversion story is so well known and because we have read so many of his New Testament writings, we forget what his early life before Jesus was like. I want you to recall someone today who hates Christianity, who mocks and persecutes or even delights at the killing of Christians, yet thinks they have the fullness of truth (even if that is atheism, ironically). If that person had a radical encounter with Jesus Christ, people would be shocked, possibly still afraid, and skeptical of the truth of their conversion. This is what happened with Paul. Here are a few key events before his conversion:

- Saul was present at the death of St. Stephen, the first martyr, who was stoned to death. "Then they cast [Stephen]
  out of the city and stoned him; and the witnesses laid
  down their garments at the feet of a young man named
  Saul" (Acts 7:58). As St. Stephen died, "Saul was consent-
  ing to his death" (Acts 8:1).

- Saul terrorized the Church. Following the death of St.
  Stephen, "a great persecution arose against the church
  in Jerusalem; and they were all scattered throughout the
  region of Judea and Samar'ia, except the apostles. Devout
  men buried Stephen, and made great lamentation over
  him. But Saul laid waste the church, and entering house
  after house, he dragged off men and women and committed them to prison" (Acts 8:1–3).

- Saul ratted out and imprisoned Christians: "But Saul, still
  breathing threats and murder against the disciples of the
  Lord, went to the high priest and asked him for letters
  to the synagogues at Damascus, so that if he found any
  belonging to the Way, men or women, he might bring
  them bound to Jerusalem" (Acts 9:1–2).

Even reading this now, we find these evil acts of St. Paul's
former life chilling and terrifying. This man, filled with anger
and hatred, dragged people out of their houses to imprison
or murder them because of their faith in Jesus Christ. Let's
read what happens next:

Now as he journeyed he approached Damascus, and suddenly a light from heaven flashed about him. And he fell to the ground and heard a voice saying to him, "Saul, Saul, why do you persecute me?" And he said, "Who are you, Lord?" And he said, "I am Jesus, whom you are persecuting; but rise and enter the city, and you will be told what you are to do." The men who were traveling with him stood speechless, hearing the voice but seeing no one. Saul arose from the ground; and when his eyes were opened, he could see nothing; so they led him by the hand and brought him into Damascus. And for three days he was without sight, and neither ate nor drank.

Now there was a disciple at Damascus named Anani'as. The Lord said to him in a vision, "Anani'as." And he said, "Here I am, Lord." And the Lord said to him, "Rise and go to the street called Straight, and inquire in the house of Judas for a man of Tarsus named Saul; for behold, he is praying, and he has seen a man named Anani'as come in and lay his hands on him so that he might regain his sight." But Anani'as answered, "Lord, I have heard from many about this man, how much evil he has done to your saints at Jerusalem; and here he has authority from the chief priests to bind all who call upon your name." But the Lord said to him, "Go, for he is a chosen instrument of mine to carry my name before the Gentiles and kings and the sons of

Israel; for I will show him how much he must suffer
for the sake of my name." So Anani'as departed and
entered the house. And laying his hands on him he
said, "Brother Saul, the Lord Jesus who appeared
to you on the road by which you came, has sent me
that you may regain your sight and be filled with
the Holy Spirit." And immediately something like
scales fell from his eyes and he regained his sight.
Then he rose and was baptized, and took food and
was strengthened. (Acts 9:3–19)

Immediately after this, Paul started preaching in the
synagogue that Jesus "is the Son of God" (Acts 9:20). Some
of the apostles were still confused and scared, questioning
whether this conversion was real (Acts 9:26), but as people
heard Paul preach, they were "amazed" and "confounded" at
what God had done through him. And as the Lord promised
("I will show him how much he must suffer for the sake of
my name"), Paul experienced imprisonment, a thorn in his
side, scourgings and beatings, and being shipwrecked. Yet he
wrote letters to various Christian communities encouraging
them and sharing with them what God has done and what
God can do.

The book of Revelation tells us that the devil will be
conquered by the "blood of the lamb and by the word of
their testimony" (Rv 12:11). The testimony of one who has
been transformed by Christ is powerful! Paul's conversion
and resulting witness spurred many additional conversions

to Christianity. Wherever he went, even though there were strong forces trying to quiet him, people who heard his testimony were amazed and confounded to the point of conviction.

God wants you to share your transformation, too! Whether you are in the grocery store, at work, at school, at a restaurant, or on social media, you never know how your witness of God's love changing your life could impact one soul (or even hundreds, thousands, or millions!). Your story, which is unique to you, may also be familiar and encouraging to others. Your witness of how you overcame addiction or how you deal with pride or how you cope with anxiety or how you deal with suffering, all because of God's work in your life and the grace he gives you, can be a massive balm to a world that is wounded and hurting. And as I know with my own conversion, this kind of work is never one and done—God is always transforming our hearts, every day, deeper and deeper, as we allow the master goldsmith to refine us with his fiery love so that we might be free, so that we can say with St. Paul: "I have been crucified with Christ; it is no longer I who live, but Christ who lives in me; and the life I now live in the flesh I live by faith in the Son of God, who loved me and gave himself for me" (Gal 2:20).

Pray

God, thank you for the witness of St. Paul and all the saints who have gone before me. Their lives show me that with you "all things are possible," and that no one is ever "too far gone." Transform me *every day*, Lord, and help me to be a new creation! I pray for all those in my life who need graces of faith, hope, love, humility, peace, and joy—pour those graces upon them now, and help me be a testimony to them of your love and your light!

Ponder

* How has God transformed your life in big or small ways? Are there areas where you have experienced victory? Or are there vices (like pride, sloth, envy, lust, anger, etc.) that have lessened through the combination of God's grace and your habitual choosing of the good?

* Who is the most inspiring person or saint you can relate to? How can they mentor you on the journey to heaven?

* Who in your life needs to hear the Good News through you? How can your testimony inspire others to let God transform them?

Memorize

Choose one or more primary or secondary verses to work on this week or this month. Head to "Let's Memorize Scripture!" on page xxii to select a method to help you memorize your choices.

One

For freedom

Christ has set us free;

stand fast therefore,
and do not submit again to a
yoke of slavery.

GALATIANS 5:1

Two

Therefore, if anyone is in
Christ, he is a new creation;
the old has passed away,

behold, the new has come.

2 CORINTHIANS 5:17

Three

A new heart
I will give you,

and a new spirit I will
put within you; and I will
take out of your flesh the
heart of stone and give
you a heart of flesh.

EZEKIEL 36:26

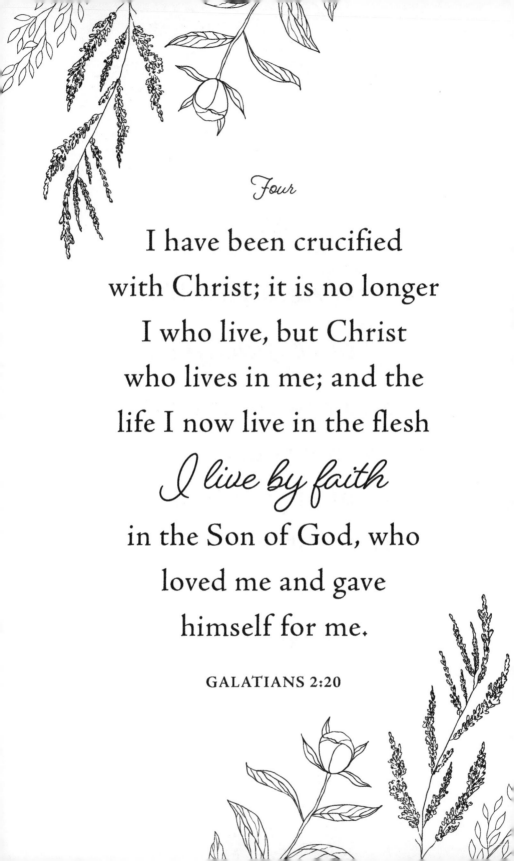

Four

I have been crucified
with Christ; it is no longer
I who live, but Christ
who lives in me; and the
life I now live in the flesh
I live by faith
in the Son of God, who
loved me and gave
himself for me.

GALATIANS 2:20

ALTERNATIVE VERSES

Five

Remember not the former things,
    nor consider the things of old.
Behold, I am doing a new thing;
    now it springs forth, do you not perceive it?
I will make a way in the wilderness
    and rivers in the desert.

ISAIAH 43:18–19

Six

But now put them all away: anger, wrath, malice, slander, and foul talk from your mouth. Do not lie to one another, seeing that you have put off the old nature with its practices and have put on the new nature, which is being renewed in knowledge after the image of its creator.

COLOSSIANS 3:8–10

Seven

And he who sat upon the throne said, "Behold,
I make all things new." Also he said, "Write this,
for these words are trustworthy and true."

REVELATION 21:5

Eight

So if the Son makes you free, you will be free
indeed.

JOHN 8:36

Nine

Put off your old nature which belongs to your
former manner of life and is corrupt through
deceitful lusts, and be renewed in the spirit of
your minds, and put on the new nature, created
after the likeness of God in true righteousness
and holiness.

EPHESIANS 4:22–24

Ten

We were buried therefore with him by baptism into death, so that as Christ was raised from the dead by the glory of the Father, we too might walk in newness of life.

ROMANS 6:4

Using the space provided, write down your memory verse in different ways—in cursive, a fancy script, or in your everyday handwriting. Use different media—markers, colored pencils, sharpies, or watercolor in a notebook or on paper.

SEVEN

Life in the Holy Spirit

A new life in Christ requires a life in the Holy Spirit. Why? Because Jesus gave us his Spirit—the same spirit that raised him from the dead—so we might be little Christs ("Christians") and be like him. Without the Holy Spirit, we cannot be like Christ. And there is no other religion in the world that claims something like this—the God of the universe became man, died for the sins of the world, and then gives every follower of his the same Spirit he had. Wow!

The Holy Spirit is the love of the Father and the Son. St. Paul said that "God's love has been poured into our hearts through the Holy Spirit who has been given to us" (Rom 5:5). The Holy Spirit is the one who makes us holy. The Holy Spirit is the one who moves us from living in the flesh and being enslaved to the things of the flesh (like drunkenness, immorality, impurity, jealousy, anger, selfishness, dissension, idolatry) to living a life that bears the fruits of the Spirit: "love, joy, peace, patience, kindness, goodness, faithfulness, gentleness, [and] self-control" (Gal 5:19–23). This Holy Spirit not only infuses grace into our souls to "heal it of sin and sanctify it" (CCC, 1999) but also invites us into God's family as adopted sons and daughters ("for you did not receive the spirit of slavery to fall back into fear, but you have received the spirit of sonship" [Rom 8:15]).

Is it possible to be baptized and raised Catholic and not live a life in the Holy Spirit? Absolutely! Just look at the disciples before Pentecost. They were baptized and had followed Jesus for years, yet they still doubted and hid themselves in fear after Jesus's death and Resurrection. In the upper room, though, when the Holy Spirit fell on them like tongues of fire, they were filled with a new zeal and courage. They started to do amazing things, from healing people in the name of Jesus (one person was even healed by St. Peter's shadow in Acts 5:15) to raising people from the dead to courageously preaching the Gospel even to the point of death!

In the past, I lived a life of spiritual mediocrity and laziness, pride, lust, anger, and selfishness. The Holy Spirit I received in Baptism and was sealed with in Confirmation was more like a tiny pilot light flickering in me than a raging fire of love and grace. St. Paul says to Timothy, "I remind you to stir into flame the gift of God that you have through the imposition of my hands. For God did not give us a spirit of cowardice but rather of power and love and self-control" (2 Tm 1:6–7, NAB). When we have a conversion or learn about life in the Holy Spirit, we become receptive to letting that fire of love be stirred up in our hearts and souls. We let go of control and let the Holy Spirit take over, for he is like the wind: "The wind blows where it wills, and you hear the sound of it, but you do not know whence it comes or whither it goes; so it is with every one who is born of the Spirit" (Jn 3:8). That is a little scary for any of us who are control freaks. We can't control the Holy Spirit. When you walk in the Holy Spirit, you never know what will happen, who you will encounter, or the miracles that will occur.

When you live a life in the Holy Spirit, you may hear God speak or even ask you to do things you never thought you would do. What, Lord? You want me to give my testimony in front of people? I'm terrified of that! You want me to volunteer to do *what* for you? I'm not capable! You want me to pray with that person for their healing? Heck, no! You want me to say *what* to that person? I'll look so silly! Yet, when we are obedient to the voice of God, and do what he asks of us with a leap of faith, we will experience miracles and become bolder with each leap.

We are given the Holy Spirit for two reasons: our own holiness and for building up the Body of Christ. Many people have natural gifts and talents like singing, teaching, or preaching, but the charisms we are given through Baptism are *supernatural* gifts (many of which build on our natural talents) that help others encounter the living Christ. St. Paul talks about the charisms in 1 Corinthians 12, sharing that "there are varieties of gifts, but the same Spirit" (v. 4) and that "to each is given the manifestation of the Spirit for the common good" (v. 7). The *Catechism* says,

> Whether extraordinary or simple and humble, charisms are graces of the Holy Spirit which directly or indirectly benefit the Church, ordered as they are to her building up, to the good of men, and to the needs of the world. Charisms are to be accepted with gratitude by the person who receives them and by all members of the Church as well. They are a wonderfully rich grace for the apostolic vitality and for the holiness of the entire Body of Christ, provided they really are genuine gifts of the Holy Spirit and are used in full conformity with authentic promptings of this same Spirit, that is, in keeping with charity, the true measure of all charisms. (799–800)

These charisms are *not* dependent on our holiness. That's why St. Paul says that "if I have prophetic powers, and understand all mysteries and all knowledge, and if I have all faith, so as to remove mountains, but have not love, I am nothing" (1 Cor 13:2). This is evidenced by the many times we have seen famous preachers, teachers, or healers with successful public ministries turn out to be privately leading lives of mortal sin. They may have been blessed with abundant charisms, but they fell short of fulfilling the part of 1 Corinthians 13 where Paul essentially says that we need to let the love of God penetrate our hearts so that the charisms are not just a show but a demonstration of what is happening in our hearts.

So what are some of the charisms named by St. Paul in 1 Corinthians 12? There are charisms of faith (if you know God can move mountains, you have this gift), wisdom (my eight-year-old is wiser than many eighty-year-olds I know), prophecy (which is not telling the future, but reminding people of who they are—children of God—and what they're made for—heaven), discernment of spirits (sometimes it's seeing things not of this world like angels or demons, but often it's having a sense that something or someone is either peaceful or massively "off"), speaking in tongues and interpreting tongues (this is when you speak a language you don't know and there's someone who interprets it), working miracles or mighty deeds (like Padre Pio bilocating, St. Joseph of Cupertino levitating, or St. Rita of Cascia bearing the stigmata), administration (for those of you that love spreadsheets, this is a charism! We need disciples running business offices), teaching (if you have this charism, your efforts bring people closer to Jesus, even if you're teaching something nonreligious!), preaching (this charism belongs to those who have a beautiful way of conveying, convicting, and convincing, whether or not they are ordained ministers of the Word), helping (I think of people who are deeply servant-hearted), apostleship (leading and shepherding the flock), healing (you'll never know you have this charism unless you pray for someone's healing!), and knowledge (getting a word or an image or dream or vision, often for someone else).

St. Paul rounds out his discussion of these gifts in 1 Corinthians 14, when he says, "Make love your aim, and earnestly desire the spiritual gifts, *especially that you may prophesy,*" because those who are prophets in the world speak to the Body of Christ for their "upbuilding and encouragement and consolation" (1 Cor 14:3). Our world needs prophets to remind people of heaven amid the busyness of everyday life, to remind them of their identity and their destiny, especially in a world that is hopeless and lost and enslaved by sin. You are needed in the Body of Christ, because you and your story and the charisms that God has given you are so different from me and my story and the charisms God has given me. You will reach people that I cannot reach! So, do not be afraid. Pray, "Come, Holy Spirit," whenever you don't have the words, whenever you encounter someone who needs the Gospel. Pray, "Come, Holy Spirit," when you start your day. Pray, "Come, Holy Spirit," when you are about to have a tough conversation.

Pray

Come, Holy Spirit, I consecrate this day to you. Come, Holy Spirit, fan the flame I received in my heart through Baptism. Come, Holy Spirit, help me to let go of control and give you the reins. Come, Holy Spirit, move in me, act in me, speak through me. Pour out your gifts of wisdom, knowledge, understanding, counsel, courage, piety, and fear of the Lord, and help me to live out the charisms I have received through Baptism to build up the Body of Christ. Amen.

Ponder

* When did you first hear about a life in the Holy Spirit? Did it scare you or intimidate you?

* What charisms do you think God has given you?

* How can you be more bold in your everyday walk with God?

Memorize

Choose one or more primary or secondary verses to work on this week or this month. Head to "Let's Memorize Scripture!" on page xxii to select a method to help you memorize your choices.

One

Now the Lord is the Spirit,
and where the
Spirit of the Lord is,
there is freedom.

2 CORINTHIANS 3:17

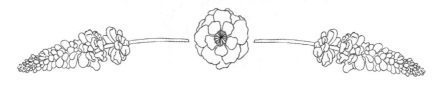

Two

But the fruit of the Spirit is
love, joy, peace,
patience, kindness,
goodness, faithfulness,
gentleness, self-control;
against such there is no law.

GALATIANS 5:22–23

Three

For this reason,
I remind you to
*stir into flame
the gift of God*
that you have through
the imposition of my
hands. For God did
not give us a spirit of
cowardice but rather
of power and love and
self-control.

2 TIMOTHY 1:6–7, NAB

Four

More than that,
we rejoice in our
sufferings, knowing that
suffering produces
endurance, and endurance
produces character, and
character produces hope,
and hope does not
disappoint us, because

*God's love has been
poured into our hearts*
through the Holy Spirit who
has been given to us.

ROMANS 5:3–5

ALTERNATIVE VERSES

Five

If the Spirit of him who raised Jesus from the dead dwells in you, he who raised Christ Jesus from the dead will give life to your mortal bodies also through his Spirit who dwells in you.

ROMANS 8:11

Six

And Peter said to them, "Repent, and be baptized every one of you in the name of Jesus Christ for the forgiveness of your sins; and you shall receive the gift of the Holy Spirit."

ACTS 2:38

Seven

And the Holy Spirit descended upon him in bodily form, as a dove, and a voice came from heaven, "Thou art my beloved Son; with thee I am well pleased."

LUKE 3:22

Eight

But the Counselor, the Holy Spirit, whom the Father will send in my name, he will teach you all things, and bring to your remembrance all that I have said to you.

JOHN 14:26

Nine

But you shall receive power when the Holy Spirit has come upon you; and you shall be my witnesses in Jerusalem and in all Judea and Samar'ia and to the end of the earth.

ACTS 1:8

Ten

Likewise the Spirit helps us in our weakness; for we do not know how to pray as we ought, but the Spirit himself intercedes for us with sighs too deep for words.

ROMANS 8:26

Practice

Practice your memory verse with a friend or spouse, and have them leave out words for you to fill in the blanks. Then you do the same for your friend! Use the space provided to practice copying your chosen verses. Write each verse at least three times.

EIGHT

God's Good Plans

When I experienced conversion as a young adult and realized, for the first time, that I had a Father in heaven who was good, who took care of me, and who had amazing plans for me, I began to trust like a child. I had always been pretty child-*ish*, but after this conversion experience, I started to become more child-*like*. I had greater dependence on God, greater trust, more awe and wonder, a greater sense of freedom like children have, less care for what other people think, and a radical surrender to God's plans for my life. I wasn't perfect then, and I'm still not perfect now. God takes us on a journey throughout our lives deeper into these things, constantly removing our unholy self-reliance, selfishness, anger, laziness, lust, and other vices and replacing them with faith, hope, love, peace, joy, humility, perseverance, and so on. But one of the major differences you can see when someone has a conversion is the radical trust they place in God. They let go of control and start living in the present. They stop living in the regrets of the past or the fear and anxiety of the future, and start living in the present day with great abandon to God's will.

When I thought about God's plans for my life, I knew, because of the Word of God, that he had good plans for me. Consider what Jesus says as he delivers the Sermon on the Mount:

> Ask, and it will be given you; seek, and you will find; knock, and it will be opened to you. For every one who asks receives, and he who seeks finds, and to him who knocks it will be opened. Or what man of you, if his son asks him for bread, will give him a stone? Or if he asks for a fish, will give him a serpent? If you then, who are evil, know how to give good gifts to your children, how much more will your Father who is in heaven give good things to those who ask him! (Mt 7:7–11)

Having confidence in who God is—a good Father—allows us to be who God calls us to be—his beloved sons and daughters. We can trust that when we pray and ask God for something, he cares. He listens. We read in the book of Jeremiah, "For I know the plans I have for you, says the LORD, plans for welfare and not for evil, to give you a future and a hope" (29:11). But many of us don't know that beyond that verse it says, "Then you will call upon me and come and pray to me, and I will hear you. You will seek me and find me; when you seek me with all your heart, I will be found by you, says the LORD" (29:12–14).

Do you believe that? That when you pray, God actually hears you? That when you seek him, you will always find him? So often we think that God doesn't really hear us or care about us, so we take matters into our own hands (like Adam and Eve). So often we pray and are disappointed that we don't get the answer we want. Or we see other people receiving answers and blessings, and we are upset or angry or envious that God isn't responding in the same way in our own lives. Singles who are praying for marriage see their peers around them getting married. Married couples who are struggling to conceive a child see their friends getting pregnant and having babies. People who are praying for success see everyone else get a lucky break but them. Ouch. It hurts to acknowledge that this envy might be in our own hearts. I can admit to you that I have more than once struggled with envy, being sad at others' blessings and rejoicing in others' failings or fallings.

So often we want the gifts more than the giver. We want *our* answers more than *the* answer. And all these things that are good—marriage, babies, success—can become idols when we place them before God or desire them more than we desire him. But there's hope for us.

When we pray for something, we can have confidence that God hears us, God receives us, and God loves us. He knows the desires of our hearts, and he delights in giving his sons and daughters good gifts. He delights in surprising us. He delights in wanting the best for us, even wanting better than what we want for ourselves.

At the bottom of all our prayers should be the desire for God. When we desire him first, everything else falls into place. When we desire him first, no matter whether the answer to our prayer is yes, no, or not yet, we still get him, and he is enough. As St. Teresa of Avila said, "Whoever has God lacks nothing; God alone is enough."

When I was in college and thinking about my future vocation, my prayer was, "God, I don't know whether you're calling me to be celibate or married, I just want you. I want to do whatever you want me to do, because I know that is what will bring the greatest joy and the greatest fruit." Even when I started writing in a journal for my "future husband" three years before I met Bobby, I often had the thought, "What if I die while I am single and my vocation is in heaven? Then, Lord, apparently I'm writing this journal for *you*, my future husband!" I would laugh at the thought, knowing that I'm not guaranteed ninety years of life on this earth. I could die tomorrow! And if that's the case, I'm ready!

Our first call, our first vocation, and God's highest plan in our life is love. When a scribe asked Jesus which commandment was the greatest, he replied, "'You shall love the Lord your God with all your heart, and with all your soul, and with all your mind, and with all your strength.' The second is this, 'You shall love your neighbor as yourself.' There is no other commandment greater than these" (Mk 12:30–31). Loving like this is what makes saints. St. Thérèse of Lisieux said, "I understood that love comprised all vocations, that love was everything, that it embraced all times and all places . . . in a word, that it was eternal!"

St. Thérèse of Lisieux is an ideal model and mentor in the ways of trusting God's good plans for our lives. I highly recommend reading her autobiography, *The Story of a Soul*, for her remarkable child-like trust shines through in every line. She truly lives out Proverbs 3:5–6: "Trust in the LORD with all your heart, and do not rely on your own insight. In all your ways acknowledge him, and he will make straight your paths." St. Thérèse died at the age of twenty-four, and I remember reading her autobiography when I was nineteen years old, thinking, "I have five more years until I'm as holy as St. Thérèse!" Well, guess what? More than twenty years later, I'm not even close! This young woman, who endured so much suffering as a child—losing her mother to breast cancer at a young age and losing five out of her nine siblings as little ones (many died as infants, but one was five years old)—still had so much faith and joy and a major charism of wisdom. Feeling a strong desire to be Jesus's bride, she

wanted to follow in the footsteps of her four older sisters
and join the convent, but the religious order and even the
bishop told her she was too young. So she went to the pope
himself to get permission! Ha! She must have read Proverbs
16:3: "Entrust your works to the LORD, and your plans will
succeed" (NAB), for she was finally allowed to enter the convent at the age of fifteen.

St. Thérèse's child-like trust in God was challenged as she
encountered other nuns who had fallen into the Jansenist way
of thinking, viewing God as a fearful judge instead of a merciful Father, a God who condemned most people to hell (or
at best, purgatory). St. Thérèse, however, had complete trust
and dependence on God, her Father. She knew that nothing
she could do could get her to heaven, but that "the elevator
which must raise me to heaven is your arms, O Jesus!" She
told one sister who struggled with fear of God (and probably
scrupulosity, which marked a lot of Jansenist thinking), "My
sister, if you look for the justice of God you will get it. The
soul will receive from God exactly what she desires." Thus, if
you desire justice, you will get justice. But if you desire mercy,
you will receive mercy!

St. Thérèse was devoted to the Little Way, espousing a
child-like trust in God and doing small, everyday things for
God with love. This way of life inspired Mother Teresa of
Calcutta many years later, who said, "I can do no great things,
only small things with great love." St. Thérèse said in *The*

Story of a Soul, "Miss no single opportunity of making some small sacrifice, here by a smiling look, there by a kindly word; always doing the smallest right and doing it all for love." She lived out this advice, even smiling and loving and offering prayers for another nun in the convent who annoyed her immensely (I'm sure there's someone in your life like this, for whom you can practice small acts of love, because I know there is in mine!).

St. Thérèse trusted God even in her battle with tuberculosis, which took her life as a young nun. Even in this suffering and her ongoing dark night of the soul, she wrote her autobiography (at the request of her prioress), dying with the words "Oh, my God, I love you!" on her lips.

My prayer and hope is that, like St. Thérèse, we place our complete trust in God our Father, who has good plans for us. Whatever those plans are, whether they include dying early or living until 105, may we love God and glorify him with all of our heart, mind, soul, and strength. May we desire him above all else, even the good things of life, for he alone is enough for us.

Pray
St. Teresa of Ávila's Guidance Prayer

Lord, grant that I may always allow myself to be guided by you, always follow your plans, and perfectly accomplish your holy will. Grant that in all things, great and small, today and all the days of my life, I may do whatever you require of me. Amen.

Ponder

* Do you trust that God has good plans for you? Why or why not?

* What is the hardest part about being child-like? In what situations are you most child-ish?

* Sometimes in our spiritual lives we err too far toward God's justice (and struggle with scrupulosity) or God's mercy (we presume that God forgives us so we just keep living a life of sin) instead of maintaining a healthy balance of the two. Which do you tend more toward, and how can you move toward the balanced middle?

✳ Do you believe that "God alone is enough"? If not, what do you desire more than God or his plans?

Memorize

Choose one or more primary or secondary verses to work on this week or this month. Head to "Let's Memorize Scripture!" on page xxii to select a method to help you memorize your choices.

One

Entrust your works
to the LORD, and

your plans will succeed.

PROVERBS 16:3, NAB

Two

Ask, and it will be given you;

seek, and you will find;

knock, and it will be opened
to you.

MATTHEW 7:7

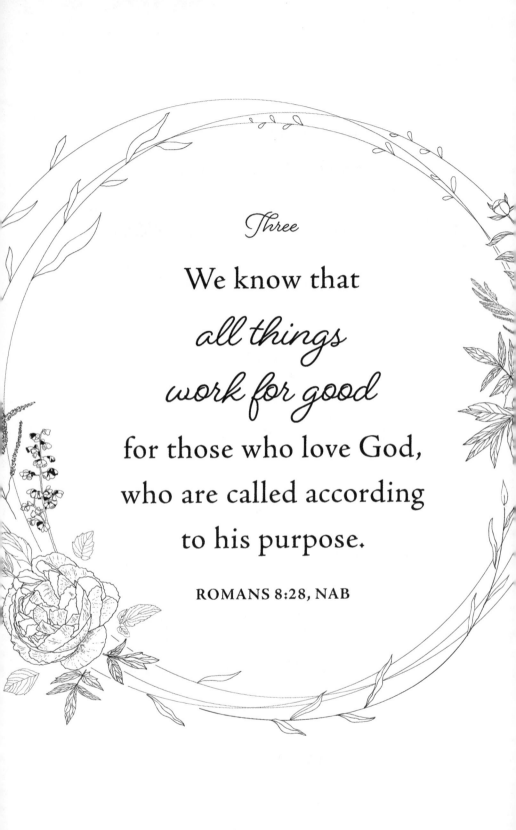

Three

We know that

all things

work for good

for those who love God,
who are called according
to his purpose.

ROMANS 8:28, NAB

Four

For I know the plans
I have for you, says
the LORD,

*plans for welfare
and not for evil,*

to give you a future
and a hope.

JEREMIAH 29:11

ALTERNATIVE VERSES

Five

Those whose steps are guided by the LORD;
whose way God approves, may stumble, but
they will never fall, for the LORD holds their
hand.

PSALM 37:23–24, NAB

Six

Trust in the LORD with all your heart, and do
not rely on your own insight. In all your ways
acknowledge him, and he will make straight
your paths.

PROVERBS 3:5–6

Seven

Before I formed you in the womb I knew you,
and before you were born I consecrated
you;
I appointed you a prophet to the nations.

JEREMIAH 1:5

Eight

A man's mind plans his way,
    but the LORD directs his steps.

PROVERBS 16:9

Nine

And I am sure that he who began a good work
in you will bring it to completion at the day of
Jesus Christ.

PHILIPPIANS 1:6

Ten

Let me hear in the morning of your merciful
    love,
    for in you I put my trust.
Teach me the way I should go,
    for to you I lift up my soul.

PSALM 143:8

Practice

Practice scripture with a group of people! Say the scripture in a circle, and each person says the next word of the scripture, one by one. Use the space provided to practice copying your chosen verses. Write each verse at least three times.

NINE

Peace

Have you ever experienced a time so beautiful and peaceful that you wanted it to last forever? Maybe you even described it as a little "slice of heaven" because it made you feel so still, so warm, so secure. For me, my honeymoon with Bobby in Kauai gave me that feeling.

First, it was one of the few times in my adult working life that I wasn't inundated with texts, calls, or emails. I didn't have to check my phone constantly to see if someone needed me or if something was due within the day or the week. Second, Kauai is one of the most gorgeous places on earth—it's called "the Garden Isle" because of its lush, rainforest climate—from the waterfalls to the mountains to the neon-colored fish and moss-green sea turtles to the warm, turquoise water. The air is warm and just humid enough to make you feel like you're being wrapped in a cinnamon roll but not so hot that you're sweating profusely. The almost daily rolling through of the summer rain shower often leaves behind a rainbow. Third, I was with the love of my life, who for the first time I got to wake up next to, make love with, and spend every minute of every day with. It was glorious. There were moments we were eating breakfast on our hotel balcony overlooking the crashing waves, enjoying our POGs (passionfruit, orange, and guava juice) with macadamia-nut pancakes and Portuguese sausage (food is my love language, if you can't tell), and I found myself wishing life could be like this forever and that this moment didn't have to end.

There have been moments in my life when I've sat in a quiet adoration chapel or sanctuary and all my anxious thoughts melted away, leaving me in the stillness of God's presence. Because I love nature so much, I have often found moments of peace at the beach or in the mountains, but I especially think of a time I wandered out of my hotel in Frankfurt, Germany, and found myself lost in a magical forest with walking paths, where the light filtered through the fall leaves, the breeze gently touched my face, and the veil between heaven and earth seemed eerily thin. They've happened when a baby (even one that isn't my own!) has fallen asleep in my arms, their sweet little breaths fluttering in and out, as their body becomes a complete deadweight in the warmth and security of my arms.

The crazy thing is that even when we're in the midst of these moments, sometimes a sadness creeps in, even maybe a pain or an ache, because we know the moment *will* end. We all long for a peace that lasts forever, not just for a moment. And we don't want peace just in heaven, we long for it now! Our lives are filled with busyness (and I once had a priest explain to me that "BUSY" stands for "Being Under Satan's Yoke," yikes!)—so much noise, so much distraction, so much chaos, so much insecurity, so much woundedness, so much expectation, and so much comparison that it might seem impossible to experience peace this side of heaven. We long for the peace that is out of this world. Is it even possible to have peace in our hearts while we are living on earth? Should we even try?

Let's take a look at what scripture tells us. St. Paul exhorts the Colossians to "let the peace of Christ rule in your hearts, to which indeed you were called in the one body" (3:15, NAB). And Jesus says in the Gospel of John, "I have said this to you, that in me you may have peace. In the world you have tribulation; but be of good cheer, I have overcome the world" (Jn 16:33). Jesus also said, "Peace I leave with you; my peace I give to you; not as the world gives do I give to you. Let not your hearts be troubled, neither let them be afraid" (Jn 14:27).

Jesus desires for us to have lives of peace, not only in heaven, but here on earth. Why? First, because God is a God of peace (Rom 15:33), and he desires to live in you. Peace is a fruit of a life lived in the Holy Spirit (Gal 5:22–23). Peace is evidence that we are secure in God and have complete trust

in God. In the Sermon on the Mount, Jesus shares these words
of encouragement and conviction:

> Therefore I tell you, do not be anxious about your
> life, what you shall eat or what you shall drink, nor
> about your body, what you shall put on. Is not life
> more than food, and the body more than clothing?
> Look at the birds of the air: they neither sow nor
> reap nor gather into barns, and yet your heaven-
> ly Father feeds them. Are you not of more value
> than they? And which of you by being anxious can
> add one cubit to his span of life? And why are you
> anxious about clothing? Consider the lilies of the
> field, how they grow; they neither toil nor spin; yet
> I tell you, even Solomon in all his glory was not
> arrayed like one of these. But if God so clothes the
> grass of the field, which today is alive and tomor-
> row is thrown into the oven, will he not much more
> clothe you, O men of little faith? Therefore do not
> be anxious, saying, "What shall we eat?" or "What
> shall we drink?" or "What shall we wear?" For the
> Gentiles seek all these things; and your heavenly
> Father knows that you need them all. But seek first
> his kingdom and his righteousness, and all these
> things shall be yours as well. Therefore do not be
> anxious about tomorrow, for tomorrow will be anx-
> ious for itself. Let the day's own trouble be sufficient
> for the day. (Mt 6:25–34)

Our Lord commands us not to be anxious or to worry about the things of this world, for he is a God who can be trusted and a God who will provide.

Second, Jesus wants us to have peace because a peaceful soul reflects God's light into the world. In his book *Searching for and Maintaining Peace: A Small Treatise on Peace of Heart*, popular retreat master Fr. Jacques Philippe gives the analogy of a soul to water. When water is agitated, the sun reflects poorly in it. But when water is still and calm, the sun reflects beautifully in it. That is like our soul. When our soul is at peace, the Son, Jesus, is reflected so brightly in it! Think of the most radiantly peaceful person you know. Then think of the most anxious person you know. What is it like to be around these people? If you are that anxious person, what do you think it is like for people to be around you?

Anxiety is common, and there are many different types of anxiety, including normal everyday anxiety, spiritual anxiety, situational anxiety, and disordered anxiety. For some of us, growing up in an unstable environment brought on a generalized anxiety. Home was a place of chaos and unrest, rather than peace and calm. Some people with anxiety experienced abuse as children or as the effect of living with an alcoholic or narcissistic parent. Divorce or abandonment by a parent or caregiver may have given rise to a feeling of insecurity or a desire for constant approval. Such underlying fears and anxieties may affect our lives even as adults.

Others deal with situational anxieties, caused by a job, a relationship, or a financial burden. When you have situational anxiety, you may wake up each day feeling like you're going to throw up or that you have a constant pit in your stomach. When you get out of that job or relationship or financial crisis, however, you may find a sense of relief.

Whatever your own situation, here are two reminders I can offer: (1) Peace in Christ *is* possible, and (2) To really deal with anxiety, it will take going to the *root cause*. Depending on the type of anxiety, some may find help by reading Fr. Philippe's book *Searching for and Maintaining Peace*; by reading something on the Catholic psychological perspective, such as Dr. Gerry Ken Crete's book *Litanies of the Heart: Relieving Post-Traumatic Stress and Calming Anxiety through Healing Our Parts*; by walking with a mentor or spiritual director; or even by working with a good professional counselor, therapist, or psychiatrist.

Pray

Jesus, pour out your grace of peace into my heart, especially when I feel agitated, worried, fearful, or anxious. You are my rock, and I am safe in your arms. Help me to be secure in you, Lord, that I may trust you with everything, for I know you are good, and I can trust you! Amen.

* What was your home environment like as a child? Was home a place of peace and calm, or anxiety and instability? Was there a specific event that ushered in a constant doubting or feeling of being "out of control"? Were you affected by a divorce or feeling of abandonment?

* Do you have a personality or temperament that is prone to anxiety? Do you see in your family history (with your mom or dad) this same struggle?

* Are you experiencing anxiety from a situation you are
  in right now, such as a job or a relationship or a financial
  burden? How can you find relief from that anxiety?

Memorize

Choose one or more primary or secondary verses to work on
this week or this month. Head to "Let's Memorize Scripture!"
on page xxii to select a method to help you memorize your
choices.

One

Cast all your anxieties on him, for

he cares about you.

1 PETER 5:7

Two

In peace I will both lie down and sleep; for you alone, O LORD, make me

dwell in safety.

PSALM 4:8

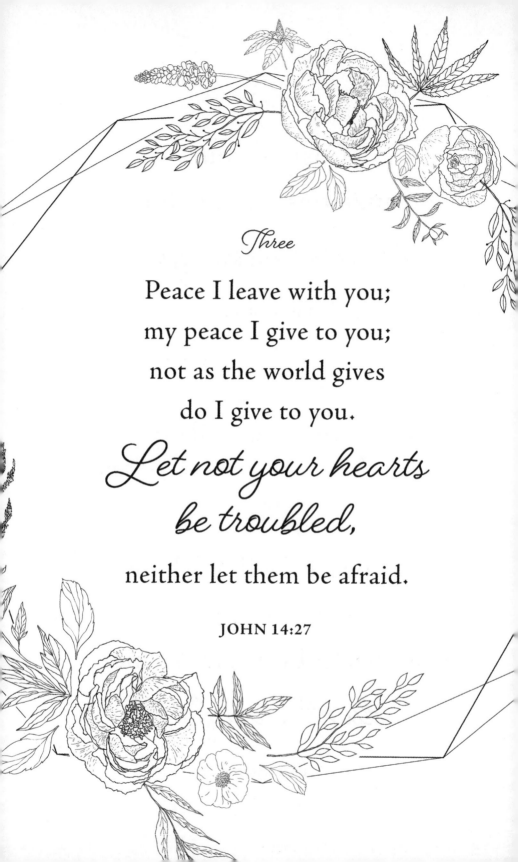

Three

Peace I leave with you;
my peace I give to you;
not as the world gives
do I give to you.

*Let not your hearts
be troubled,*

neither let them be afraid.

JOHN 14:27

Four

Have no anxiety
about anything,
but in everything

by prayer and
supplication with
thanksgiving

let your requests be made
known to God.
And the peace of God, which
passes all understanding, will
keep your hearts and your
minds in Christ Jesus.

PHILIPPIANS 4:6–7

ALTERNATIVE VERSES

Five

And let the peace of Christ control your hearts,
the peace into which you were also called in
one body. And be thankful.

COLOSSIANS 3:15, NAB

Six

I have said this to you, that in me you may have
peace. In the world you have tribulation; but
be of good cheer, I have overcome the world.

JOHN 16:33

Seven

Be still, and know that I am God. I am exalted
among the nations, I am exalted in the earth!

PSALM 46:10

Eight

May the God of hope fill you with all joy and peace in believing, so that by the power of the Holy Spirit you may abound in hope.

ROMANS 15:13

Nine

Now may the Lord of peace himself give you peace at all times in all ways. The Lord be with you all.

2 THESSALONIANS 3:16

Ten

Therefore I tell you, do not be anxious about your life, what you shall eat or what you shall drink, nor about your body, what you shall put on. Is not life more than food, and the body more than clothing? Look at the birds of the air: they neither sow nor reap nor gather into barns, and yet your heavenly Father feeds them. Are you not of more value than they? And which of you by being anxious can add one cubit to his span of life? And why are you anxious about clothing? Consider the lilies of the field, how they grow; they neither toil nor spin; yet I tell you, even Solomon in all his glory was not arrayed like one of these. But if God so clothes the grass of the field, which today is alive and tomorrow is thrown into the oven, will he not much more clothe you, O men of little faith? Therefore do not be anxious, saying, "What shall we eat?" or "What shall we drink?" or "What shall we wear?" For the Gentiles seek all these things; and your heavenly Father knows that you need them all. But seek first his kingdom and his righteousness, and all these things shall be yours as well. Therefore do not be anxious about tomorrow, for tomorrow will be anxious for itself. Let the day's own trouble be sufficient for the day.

MATTHEW 6:25–34

Practice

In a time of prayer, try to recall the most peaceful place you've been! Imagine you are there, and recite the scripture (especially the ones about peace) three times. Visualization exercises, especially where you connect a scripture with a different image (like a place), will help solidify the verse in your mind! Use the space provided to practice copying your chosen verses. Write each verse at least three times.

TEN

Forgiveness

I have a confession: I am a recovering Pharisee. I used to think I was better than other people because I had made more "sacrifices," acquired more virtue, and was more determined. I was disgusted in high school and college by Catholic friends who would go to Mass on Sunday after a Saturday night of hooking up and getting wasted. I don't know if I consciously believed it, but I'm pretty sure deep down I thought God loved me more because I went to daily Mass, went to Confession and adoration often, and said more devotions. I knew the scripture where Jesus says, "Those who are well have no need of a physician, but those who are sick. Go and learn what this means, 'I desire mercy, and not sacrifice.' For I came not to call the righteous, but sinners" (Mt 9:12–13). Nevertheless, I didn't recognize the depth of my judgment toward others, nor did I recognize the depth of my own sickness.

The apostle John asks, "How can you love God but hate your brother?" (1 Jn 4). And St. John Chrysostom calls us out by saying:

> You have tasted the Blood of the Lord, yet you do not recognize your brother. . . . You dishonor this table when you do not judge worthy of sharing your food someone judged worthy to take part in this meal. . . . God freed you from all your sins and invited you here, but you have not become more merciful. (*CCC*, 1397, quoting St. John Chrysostom, Hom. in 1 Cor. 27, 4: PG 61, 229–30; cf. Mt 25:40)

Ouch. There have been many times I've attended Mass and just gone through the motions and not allowed the graces to penetrate my heart. And I know that sometimes I've left Mass and immediately gotten angry with a family member or yelled at the person who cut me off in traffic or rashly judged a friend's choices.

That's why it's beautiful (and so important) that at the beginning of Mass, we ask God to have mercy on us—"*Kyrie, Eleison* (Lord, have mercy), *Christe Eleison* (Christ, have mercy), *Kyrie Eleison* (Lord, have mercy)." We ask the Lord to forgive our sins so that our hearts may be in the proper disposition to receive him in Holy Communion. And thank God for the Sacrament of Reconciliation! The *Catechism* states that "by receiving more frequently through this sacrament the gift of the Father's mercy, we are spurred to be merciful as he is merciful" (1458). That's exactly what needed to happen to me—to be more merciful as he is merciful.

I can't pinpoint a lightbulb moment when the Lord showed me the state of my heart, but I know that allowing the Lord to heal my wounds has opened me to receive the wounds of others more compassionately. The more I came to recognize that I am not perfect, the more I saw that I am tempted and the more my understanding and love for the people I once judged grew.

You probably know the saying "hurt people hurt people," but the flip side is also true: healed people heal people. When we are hurt or wounded, we operate out of that state with defense mechanisms based on the lies we believe about ourselves. One of my favorite resources to share with people is Bob Schucht's book *Be Healed*, in which he discusses the "Seven Deadly Wounds" and the lies that come from them. Serving in ministry for more than twenty-two years and hearing the stories of thousands of people from middle-school age to the elderly, I have noticed patterns and defense mechanisms. For instance, I have ministered to countless young women (in my time in youth ministry and in speaking) who have a poor or even horrific relationship with their father, who then turn to men (oftentimes in unhealthy and unchaste romantic relationships) to seek affirmation and love. I have also encountered men both young and old who present themselves with a tough-guy demeanor, only to find out that behind the facade there is an insecure or scared man who was told he was worthless or a failure. It wasn't until reading *Be Healed* that I realized that these defense mechanisms, or "fruit of the actions," come from a much deeper root of woundedness. Even with myself, I used to go to the Sacrament of Confession to chop off the fruits of anger, lust, sloth, pride, envy, and so on, but I always failed to address the root and ask myself, "Why is it that you do this thing? Why do you get angry when X happens? Why do you gossip? Why are you selfish in these moments?" And you know what happens when you chop off the fruit but don't pull out the root? It grows right back like a weed that has been snipped and not pulled.

As with anxiety, we must address the root cause, bring it to the light, and allow for healing. When we allow Jesus to heal us of our woundedness, we in turn become more merciful. *Mercy*, which is *misericordia* in Latin, comes from the root words "misery" and "heart." Allowing Jesus to heal our hearts that are in misery enables us to "commiserate" and have a heart of mercy toward others who are in misery. I'm not only talking about the people we judge or have wounded; I'm also talking about the people who have badly wounded us. Those people who abandoned us, rejected us, used us, abused us, cheated on, or betrayed us? They also are massively wounded. Their actions came from a heart in misery. And I know that one of the hardest things to do is heed the call to forgive and to have mercy on those people and to love those people as Christ loves them.

When we experience rejection, abandonment, fear, or shame at the hands of another, we often carry around the resulting resentment, anger, or unforgiveness in our hearts toward that person. There is so much pain surrounding those wounds, and we feel like we have some sense of control when we hang on to the hatred we feel toward the person who wounded us. The truth is, though, that this unforgiveness doesn't give us power or control, but in fact eats away at our soul. My husband Bobby often uses the analogy of Gollum in *Lord of the Rings*, a hobbit who has withered away into a goblin-like being due to his obsession with the Ring, which captivates and imprisons him. He knows it is killing him, but he can't let go of it. It's too painful. It has become a part of him, even changing who he is.

Every time we pray the Our Father, we ask God to "forgive us our trespasses *as we forgive* those who trespass against us." Yikes. We are actually telling the Lord *not* to forgive us when we haven't forgiven someone in our own life. That's why unforgiveness is a block to healing. We can't receive God's mercy if we haven't extended mercy. Forgiveness isn't saying that what someone did to you was okay. No, it's actually acknowledging that what they did to you was *not* okay. It's admitting that you were supposed to experience *love*, but you experienced a lack of love or a distortion of love at the hands of that person. But instead of doling out your own vengeance upon them, you want to be free of them and thus you give them and their outcome to God, so that he can deal with them in his justice and his mercy.

Forgiving also doesn't mean forgetting. As the *Catechism* says, "It is not in our power not to feel or to forget an offense; but the heart that offers itself to the Holy Spirit turns injury into compassion and purifies the memory in transforming the hurt into intercession" (2843). Wow. Forgiveness doesn't mean not feeling pain! But, in offering our woundedness to the Holy Spirit, we can have compassion for the person who hurt us (realizing the depths of their own woundedness) and intercede for them. Let us practice that now, as we do an exercise of forgiveness.

Place yourself in the presence of God, taking a few deep breaths in and out. Ask God to pour out upon you his graces of faith, hope, love, healing, peace, and mercy. Think of a person who hurt you and causes you pain still to this day. If there are many people, start with just one. Recount what they did to you, what they took from you, how they wounded you. And then take them in your hands and offer them to God to be dealt with in his justice and his mercy.

Ask the Lord to give you the grace to forgive. Ask the Lord to give you the graces of compassion and understanding, to see this offender as a child who was once himself or herself abused, abandoned, neglected, rejected, or wounded. Then finish your prayer by interceding for this person with a Hail Mary, asking for their conversion and the healing of their wounds.

Lord, your steadfast love never ceases. You offer me constant forgiveness, and yet I struggle to do this for others. Grant me the graces of compassion and understanding so that I can forgive as you have taught me. Amen.

* How has the Lord forgiven you in small and big ways?

* Are there any parts of your heart that judge others? Are
  there specific sins of others that make you feel like you
  are better than them?

* Who in your life has been the hardest person to forgive
  and why?

✶ What wounds and lies do you need to address in your
own heart? When did these wounds happen (was it in
childhood?), and when did these lies first enter your
mind?

Memorize

Choose one or more primary or secondary verses to work on
this week or this month. Head to "Let's Memorize Scripture!"
on page xxii to select a method to help you memorize your
choices.

One

Be merciful,

even as
your Father is merciful.

LUKE 6:36

Two

Let us then with confidence

draw near to the

throne of grace,

that we may receive mercy
and find grace to help
in time of need.

HEBREWS 4:16

Three

The steadfast love of
the Lord never ceases,

*his mercies never
come to an end;*

they are new every
morning; great is
your faithfulness.

LAMENTATIONS 3:22–23

Four

Have mercy on me, O God,
according to your
merciful love;

*according to your
abundant mercy
blot out my
transgressions.*

Wash me thoroughly from my
iniquity,
and cleanse me from my sin!

PSALM 51:1–2

ALTERNATIVE VERSES

Five

Surely goodness and mercy shall follow me all the days of my life; and I shall dwell in the house of the LORD for ever.

PSALM 23:6

Six

But when he heard it, he said, "Those who are well have no need of a physician, but those who are sick. Go and learn what this means, 'I desire mercy, and not sacrifice.' For I came not to call the righteous, but sinners."

MATTHEW 9:12–13

Seven

Blessed are the merciful, for they shall obtain mercy.

MATTHEW 5:7

Eight

But God, who is rich in mercy, out of the great love with which he loved us, even when we were dead through our trespasses, made us alive together with Christ (by grace you have been saved), and raised us up with him, and made us sit with him in the heavenly places in Christ Jesus, that in the coming ages he might show the immeasurable riches of his grace in kindness toward us in Christ Jesus.

EPHESIANS 2:4–7

Nine

Forbearing one another and, if one has a complaint against another, forgiving each other; as the Lord has forgiven you, so you also must forgive.

COLOSSIANS 3:13

Ten

If we confess our sins, he is faithful and just, and will forgive our sins and cleanse us from all unrighteousness.

1 JOHN 1:9

Recite your memory verse every day, but also review your previously memorized ones! Pick a day of the week to be your "review day," and go over your older verses to keep them at the forefront of your mind. Use the space provided to practice copying your chosen verses. Write each verse at least three times.

ELEVEN

Gratitude

St. Paul tells the Thessalonians to "rejoice always, pray constantly, give thanks in all circumstances; for this is the will of God in Christ Jesus for you" (1 Thes 5:16–18). I'm sure you have wondered, just as I have, if that is actually possible. Is it possible to rejoice always and give thanks in every circumstance? Is it possible to give thanks to God when we are undergoing sickness or chronic pain? Death of a loved one? Loss of a job? Adultery or betrayal? Infertility or miscarriage? Is it really possible to rejoice in those times and be grateful in those circumstances?

When I find myself wondering about these things, I turn to the saints. These are the mentors who have gone before us to show us how to live the Christian life. They are the "cloud of witnesses" who have persevered while "looking to Jesus the pioneer and perfecter of our faith, who for the joy that was set before him endured the cross, despising the shame, and is seated at the right hand of the throne of God" (Heb 12:1–2). They are the ones who are not without sin, but just like us with all our flaws and different temperaments and temptations. They are the ones who show us what is possible as a human in the natural world operating with God and his supernatural grace. Some of them lost *everything*—even their lives—and still praised God with thanksgiving and gratitude.

The majority of the canonized saints lived before the ideas of positive psychology took hold. Those who work in positive psychology study gratitude and how it rewires the brain. The saints lived what positive psychology found—that gratitude makes you happier psychologically (by enhancing your mood and bringing more positive thoughts and emotions), improves your bodily health (by giving you a stronger immune system, better sleep, and better cardiac functioning), and makes you more likable socially (by strengthening your relationships, making you more empathic, and encouraging better communication).

I love when science proves what our faith has taught all along! While positive psychology shows what gratitude *does*, the saints show us how to *be* grateful, especially in the midst of suffering. They show us that gratitude is not only possible in the Christian life but necessary, and it leads to happiness—and in our case as Christians, it leads us to the supreme happiness, which is God. God is also the *source* of our happiness and gratitude. It's like a never-ending cycle of goodness! God is the reason we are grateful, and being grateful to God leads us back to him, our ultimate happiness.

I know that in my own life I need the reminder to be grateful. In my selfishness and sense of entitlement, I often get bogged down with complaining and seeing the worst of things. Let us walk with the saints in their journeys of gratitude, which will hopefully inspire in us a greater desire and inclination toward thanksgiving.

If we go back to the early church and look at St. Paul's experience, we find that for the sake of Christ, he was beaten, stoned, scourged, shipwrecked, and betrayed. I mean, I complain if the Wi-Fi on the plane doesn't work. Yet St. Paul rejoices and gives thanks *while in prison* and says, "Whatever you do, in word or in deed, do everything in the name of the Lord Jesus, giving thanks to God the Father through him" (Col 3:17). Rather than sitting in prison wallowing in his sadness, St. Paul actively encourages others and writes letters to the Colossians, the Ephesians, the Philippians, and Philemon.

St. Paul knows that his suffering inspires his fellow Christians, as he writes to the people of Philippi: "I thank God in all my remembrance of you, always in every prayer of mine for you all making my prayer with joy, thankful for your partnership in the gospel from the first day until now . . . I want you to know . . . most of the brethren have been made confident in the Lord because of my imprisonment, and are much more bold to speak the word of God without fear" (Phil 1:3–5, 14).

St. Paul's witness and writings were encouraging his fellow Christians then, and they are still encouraging us today to have greater faith, courage, hope, and gratitude.

Another early church saint who showed gratitude and joy (and even a sense of humor) while undergoing persecution was St. Lawrence. I am grateful that his feast day, August 10, is also my wedding anniversary because I greatly admire anyone who has a good sense of humor, and I agree with Mother Teresa of Calcutta that "joy is the net of love by which we catch souls." St. Lawrence was persecuted and killed alongside Pope Sixtus II and three other deacons under the Roman emperor Valerian (253–260). According to tradition, while St. Lawrence was being roasted to death, he made the comment, "Now you may turn me over. My body is roasted enough on this side." Then, as he was close to death, he offered gratitude to the Lord while saying, "I thank you, O Lord, that I am permitted to enter your portals." I hope that one day, if I'm ever roasted to death, I can have the same attitude as St. Lawrence!

One of my favorite modern-day women on the path to sainthood is Chiara "Luce" Badano, who also reflected great gratitude and joy in the midst of immense suffering. Born in 1971, she was the long-awaited and only child of a couple who had tried to conceive for eleven years. While Chiara appeared to be a normal teenager who loved sports and pop music and hanging out with her friends, her involvement with her faith (especially within the Italian movement called

Focolare) and her love for Jesus made her wise beyond her years. At the age of seventeen, she was diagnosed with a cancerous tumor in the bone. Throughout surgery and even chemotherapy, Chiara was a light to all around her, including the medical staff. I've seen pictures of her with her hair gone because of the chemotherapy, talking on the phone in her bed with the most radiant smile on her face, and thought to myself, "That kind of smile in the midst of suffering doesn't come from the newest tech gadget or popularity or money. That comes from Jesus!"

As Chiara drew close to death, after two years of fighting bone cancer, she chose not to have an increase in morphine because she wanted to stay coherent and offer Jesus her pain. After one intense night of suffering, she told her mom that she offered all her pain to Jesus. Chiara started planning her own funeral, choosing the songs and the flowers and even what she was going to wear. She decided she wanted to be buried in a wedding dress because she knew that in heaven she would be married to Jesus. Realizing that it would be hard for her mother to prepare her only daughter to be buried, she encouraged her mother by saying, "When you get me ready, you will have to repeat—now Chiara Luce sees Jesus." Chiara died in 1990 at the age of nineteen and was declared "Blessed" by Pope Benedict XVI in 2010. Her witness proves that youth does not mean less wisdom and that suffering does not mean less joy.

There are many other saints who maintained gratitude, hope, and love for God in the midst of suffering, such as St. Monica (who suffered through a terrible marriage), St. John of the Cross (who suffered a dark night of the soul), St. Thomas More (who suffered political persecution and martyrdom), and St. Gianna Beretta Molla (who suffered illness during pregnancy and refused to abort her child, instead laying down her life for her baby, dying within a week of giving birth). But I want to share one last story with you of a man named Venerable Cardinal Francis Xavier Nguyen Van Thuan.

While Bobby and I were on our ten-year-anniversary trip to Rome a few years ago, we decided to have a very loose itinerary, just stumbling into whatever churches came into our path, since we had been to Rome on other occasions and had gone to all the "must-see" churches and tourist destinations like the Colosseum and Trevi Fountain. One day, we ventured to Trastevere at the encouragement of a friend, who said the neighborhood was beautiful and the food was especially good. Walking around, we kept coming across church after beautiful church. These little churches were absolutely stunning and yet completely empty.

One church we entered was called Chiesa di Santa Maria della Scala. As we admired all the beautiful side altars, we saw a poster of Venerable Cardinal Francis Xavier Nguyen Van Thuan. We thought nothing of it (many churches have posters or advertisements for different saints or events) until I attempted to read the Italian placard on the wall and writing on the nearby tomb (my high school French and minuscule Spanish vocabulary helped with that). When I told Bobby that Cardinal Van Thuan was actually buried there, he couldn't believe it. The same Cardinal Van Thuan whose book Bobby had just read and shared with me! The same Cardinal Van Thuan who was captured by Communists in Vietnam and spent *nine years* (out of thirteen in prison) in solitary confinement, celebrating Mass in his hand, with only a host and a few drops of wine that had been smuggled in to him. I can't imagine staying sane in solitary confinement for a day, let alone nine years, and I definitely can't imagine being grateful, yet Cardinal Van Thuan said, "Thanks to God's help, I have never regretted my destiny." This man, who at first struggled with hopelessness, having been arrested under false pretenses and knowing that no one was coming to save him, united himself to the Cross and was filled with the peace that only God can give, choosing to "live in the present moment, filling it to the brim with love." In 1988, he was finally released from prison, brought to Rome by Pope John Paul II (who made him a cardinal), and lived out the remainder of his life there. He died in 2002 and was buried in the little church in Trastevere.

When I read the lives of the saints, who have mentored me in my journey of faith, I am inspired and know that it is actually possible to "do everything in the name of the Lord

Jesus, giving thanks to God the Father through him" (Col 3:17). Gratitude is not dependent on circumstance; it is dependent on God living in and through us. And I know I want that!

Jesus, pour out the grace of gratitude into my heart. Help me in every moment to be thankful for the gift of life, the gift of your love, and ultimately the gift of being one with you in heaven! Help me to do everything with thanksgiving, even when I am sad or suffering, and place the saints at the forefront of my mind to mentor me in gratitude! St. Paul, pray for me. Bl. Chiara "Luce" Badano, pray for me! Venerable Cardinal Francis Xavier Nguyen Van Thuan, pray for me!

Ponder

* Who is the greatest witness of gratitude in the midst of suffering in your life?

* Think of a time when you suffered greatly. Did you experience or not experience gratitude in the midst of it?

* What are you most grateful for in your life?

✶ How do you recount gratitude throughout the day? Do you say it out loud to people around you or have a gratitude journal?

Memorize

Choose one or more primary or secondary verses to work on this week or this month. Head to "Let's Memorize Scripture!" on page xxii to select a method to help you memorize your choices.

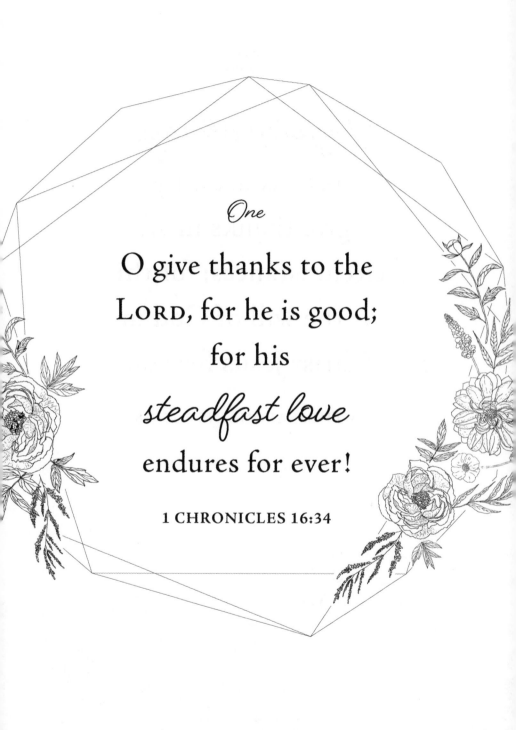

One

O give thanks to the
Lord, for he is good;
for his

steadfast love

endures for ever!

1 CHRONICLES 16:34

Two

Rejoice always,

pray constantly,
give thanks in all
circumstances; for this
is the will of God in
Christ Jesus for you.

1 THESSALONIANS 5:16–18

Three

It is good to give thanks to
the LORD,
to sing praises to your
name, O Most High;
to declare your

merciful love

in the morning,
and your faithfulness
by night.

PSALM 92:1–2

Four

Let the word of Christ dwell
in you richly, as you teach
and admonish one another
in all wisdom, and as you
sing psalms and hymns
and spiritual songs with
thankfulness in your hearts
to God. And whatever you do,
in word or deed, do everything
in the name of the Lord
Jesus, giving thanks to
God the Father through him.

COLOSSIANS 3:16–17

ALTERNATIVE VERSES

Five

O come, let us sing to the LORD;
let us make a joyful noise to the rock of our
salvation!
Let us come into his presence with thanksgiving;
let us make a joyful noise to him with songs
of praise!
For the LORD is a great God,
and a great King above all gods.

PSALM 95:1–3

Six

Continue steadfastly in prayer, being watchful
in it with thanksgiving.

COLOSSIANS 4:2

Seven

But thanks be to God, who gives us the victory
through our Lord Jesus Christ.

1 CORINTHIANS 15:57

Eight

Therefore let us be grateful for receiving a kingdom that cannot be shaken, and thus let us offer to God acceptable worship, with reverence and awe; for our God is a consuming fire.

HEBREWS 12:28–29

Nine

Enter his gates with thanksgiving,
and his courts with praise!
Give thanks to him, bless his name!

PSALM 100:4

Ten

For everything created by God is good, and nothing is to be rejected if it is received with thanksgiving; for then it is consecrated by the word of God and prayer.

1 TIMOTHY 4:4–5

Practice

Print out scripture verses (whether of your own design or someone else's), and hang them up to see them often. In my house, we put them in clear sheet protectors and connect them with a key ring and hang them on a thumbtack on the wall where we can see them from the kitchen and the couch—the places we hang out most often! Use the space provided to practice copying your chosen verses. Write each verse at least three times.

TWELVE

Longing for God

Back when I was a twenty-two-year-old youth minister in Ventura, California, I was sitting on my bed one night with my heart aching for God to bring me my future husband. "God, you are God of the universe. You can do anything! I know you love me and give me good gifts. Bring me my husband now," I cried out with abandon and a wink. I decided to play the ridiculous game of Bible roulette, where you open the Bible to a random place and put your finger on a passage. This is a terrible idea, by the way, because there are weird passages in scripture like 2 Kings 2:22, where a she-bear comes out of the forest and tears forty-two children to pieces, or like Psalm 38:7, where the psalmist cries that his loins burn with fever (which probably would have been an appropriate verse to land on for my situation that day). Thank God, though, I landed on Psalm 63, which is a psalm often prayed in the Liturgy of the Hours (a book of multi-day prayers that every

religious sister and brother and priest commits to pray daily).
I started reading the psalm slowly:

> O God, you are my God—for you I long!
> For you my body yearns;
>   for you my soul thirsts,
> Like a land parched, lifeless,
>   and without water.
> So I look to you in the sanctuary
>   to see your power and glory.
> For your love is better than life;
>   my lips offer you worship! (NAB)

In that moment I realized that the ache and longing of my
heart was not for a human being, but for God. It was for him
that I longed, for him that my body yearned, for him that
my soul thirsted. And where does the psalmist look? To the
sanctuary to see God's power and glory, for his love is "better
than life."

What is foreshadowed in the Old Testament is fulfilled
in the New Testament. The sanctuary we have today in our
Catholic churches is where bread and wine become the body,
blood, soul, and divinity of Jesus Christ on the altar. It is the
place where God's power and glory are revealed, as something as lowly as a piece of bread becomes the Body of Christ
through the command, "This is my body given for you."

How amazing is God's love for us! He loves us so much
that he died to save us from our sins. And as if that weren't

enough, he also gives us his very Body and Blood so that he can be *one* with us in the Eucharist. Just as there are many forms of intimacy among human beings—we can hold hands, hug, talk for hours, look each other in the eyes—we have many forms of intimacy with our God—we can praise him in song, converse with him in prayer, read his words, gaze at him in adoration. But the closest we can become with another human being while on earth is to become *one* flesh in marriage through the act of making love. And Pope Benedict XVI (then Cardinal Ratzinger) wrote in his book *The Spirit of the Liturgy*, "In the Eucharist a communion takes place that corresponds to the union of man and woman in marriage. Just as they become 'one flesh,' so in Communion we all become 'one spirit,' one person, with Christ." Wow. It is incredible that we become *one* with God! We all desire this intimacy so deeply—to be seen, known, and loved—and it is fulfilled when we receive our bridegroom Jesus Christ in the Eucharist and, ultimately, when we become one with God in heaven.

Gazing upon your beloved is amazing, but we don't want to stay there, we want to be one with them! I think of the first time I met Bobby. We were at a theology-of-the-body week-long retreat with one hundred other students. For five days, we spent six hours a day in class learning about St. John Paul II's beautiful teaching on what it means to be human, male and female. There was one session where my heart was so pierced by what I was hearing that I was on the verge of tears.

It was time for lunch, though. So I remember sitting at a table with eight other young adults, and when one of them asked why I was being so quiet (because if you know me, you know this is a rare thing), I just gestured that I needed to be quiet because God was doing something in my heart. I knew that if I spoke, the tears would become the extra salt on my plate.

During that lunch, I glanced across the table at Bobby, and he just looked at me with a gaze of love and compassion. It was like he could see into my soul. And my heart was wrecked. It felt like it tore into a thousand pieces. A year and a half later when we met again and then started dating, that gaze of love happened often. Every time, it felt like my heart was so full of love that it was about to burst. It wasn't just filled with joy; it was also filled with pain. Part of that pain is the longing to be *one* with the person you love because gazing at them is just not enough. Bobby and I waited to have sex until we were married, so that year of dating and engagement was so beautiful, yet also painful with longing to be one.

Isn't that how it feels to be here on earth, though? There's this constant longing and ache that nothing can satisfy until we finally become one with God in heaven. God knows that and therefore gives us the gift of himself, especially in the Eucharist: "The celebration of the Eucharistic sacrifice is wholly directed toward the intimate union of the faithful with Christ through communion. To receive communion is to receive Christ himself who has offered himself for us" (*CCC*, 1382).

During the season of Advent, we press into that longing as we wait for the three comings of Christ. First is the coming of Jesus as a baby at Christmas. We await this baby who was born to die, this God-man who was born in a town called Bethlehem (which means "House of Bread") and laid in a manger (which, in French, means "to eat"), all prefiguring that he would be the Bread of Life whom we would receive so we might live forever!

We await the second coming of God into our hearts every day, especially through the Eucharist. The Eucharist is a foretaste of heaven (*CCC*, 1090), a foretaste of that wedding feast where we, the Church (the bride), become one with Jesus, the bridegroom. The Mass is not just some random person's wedding; it's *your* wedding with God! Do you remember how you dressed up when you received your first Holy Communion? You dressed like a little bride or bridegroom. Every time we receive the Eucharist, we process down an aisle like a bride toward the love of our life, Jesus the bridegroom, and when we come to him, the celebrant says, "The Body of Christ," and we say, "Amen!" Essentially, in this moment, we are saying, "I do," as we then receive his Body into our body, and his Blood mingles with our blood.

Just as every time a husband and wife make love and become "one flesh" they renew their wedding vows, every time we receive Jesus in the Eucharist and become one flesh with him, we renew our vows to him (which we say earlier in the Mass through the Creed when we say, "I believe in one God"). Just as a couple at their wedding pledge to be faithful and bear fruit and give themselves totally to each other, we pledge to Jesus to be faithful to him, to bear the fruit of the Spirit, and to receive him totally and respond totally with *everything* we have and we are, holding nothing back! It's no wonder that marriage (as St. John Paul II often points out in his work *Theology of the Body*) is a sign of heavenly union, and that the Eucharistic feast is a foretaste of it.

Jesus desires intimacy with us. He says, "Abide in me, and I in you!" (Jn 15:4).

And, as we abide in him, we await his third coming at the end of time. We know not the day or the hour he will return, but with our hearts aching, we "[long] to be united with Christ, [our] Bridegroom, in the glory of heaven" (CCC, 1821) as we hope and watch and wait. St. Teresa of Avila put it so beautifully:

> Hope, O my soul, hope. You know neither the day nor the hour. Watch carefully, for everything passes quickly, even though your impatience makes doubtful what is certain, and turns a very short time into a long one. Dream that the more you struggle, the more you prove the love that you bear your God, and the more you will rejoice one day with your

Beloved, in a happiness and rapture that can never
end. (St. Teresa of Avila, Excl. 15:3, as quoted in
CCC, 1821)

Do you not desire that kind of happiness and ecstatic
rapture and love for all eternity? I know I do! My heart aches
and longs to finally be *one* with Jesus the bridegroom—who
knows me, sees me, and loves me—for all eternity! My prayer
for you as you finish this book is that the memorizing of scripture will allow the "Word of Christ [to] dwell in you richly"
(Col 3:16) and that you will experience his very Word in you
every moment of every day. And that you never forget how
good you are, loved you are, and desired you are by the King
of the Universe, the Savior of Our Souls, and the Beloved of
Our Hearts.

Whenever you feel that deep ache of your heart, pray
Psalm 63, for God is knocking on your heart desiring to be
with you, spend time with you, and hear your voice. He
wants to constantly remind you who you are and what you
are made for.

Pray

Jesus, I long for you, and I ache for the day when I can be completely one with you in heaven. Help me, when I experience that ache, to turn my desire toward you in prayer! Help me to run to you in the Eucharist when I feel lonely or weary or burdened by the ache that sometimes is so painful! You alone satisfy my heart, Lord. Thank you for your love. God, you alone are enough. Help me to know that in my mind and feel it in my heart. Amen.

Ponder

* In what ways have you experienced an "ache" for God?

* When you reflect on your past, how have you tried to satisfy that ache with things of this world?

Memorize

Choose one or more primary or secondary verses to work on this week or this month. Head to "Let's Memorize Scripture!" on page xxii to select a method to help you memorize your choices.

One

Lord,

all my longing is known
to you, my sighing is not
hidden from you.

PSALM 38:9

Two

Take delight

in the LORD, and he will
give you the desires of
your heart.

PSALM 37:4

Three

"You shall love
the Lord your God
with all your heart,
and with all your soul,
and with all your mind,
and with all your strength."
The second is this,

"You shall love your
neighbor as yourself."
There is no other
commandment
greater than
these.

MARK 12:30–31

Four

O God, you are my God—for
you I long!
For you my body yearns;
for you my soul thirsts,
Like a land parched, lifeless,
and without water.
So I look to you in the
sanctuary
to see your power and glory.

*For your love is
better than life;*
my lips offer you worship!

PSALM 63:2–4, NAB

ALTERNATIVE VERSES

Five

Whom have I in heaven but you? And there is nothing upon earth that I desire besides you.

PSALM 73:25

Six

The LORD is my shepherd, I shall not want;
    he makes me lie down in green pastures.
He leads me beside still waters;
    he restores my soul.
He leads me in paths of righteousness
    for his name's sake.

PSALM 23:1–3

Seven

The voice of my beloved!
 Behold, he comes,
    leaping upon the mountains,
    bounding over the hills.
My beloved is like a gazelle,
    or a young stag.
Behold, there he stands
    behind our wall,
    gazing in at the windows,
    looking through the lattice.
My beloved speaks and says to me:
    "Arise, my love, my fair one,
    and come away;
    for lo, the winter is past,
    the rain is over and gone.
The flowers appear on the earth,
    the time of singing has come,
    and the voice of the turtledove
    is heard in our land."

SONG OF SOLOMON 2:8–12

Eight

As the deer longs for streams of water,
  so my soul longs for you, O God.
My soul thirsts for God, the living God.
  When can I go and see the face of God?

PSALM 42:2–3, NAB

Nine

My soul longs, yes, faints
  for the courts of the LORD;
my heart and flesh sing for joy
  to the living God.

PSALM 84:2

Ten

I consider that the sufferings of this present
time are not worth comparing with the glory
that is to be revealed to us. For the creation
waits with eager longing for the revealing of
the sons of God.

ROMANS 8:18–19

Practice

Sing the scripture verse! If you can make music to the scripture or even find a song that has the scripture in it, singing it often will help you memorize the scripture so fast! Use the space provided to practice copying your chosen verses. Write each verse at least three times.

Scripture Index

NEW TESTAMENT

Jackie Angel is a Catholic speaker, singer-songwriter, worship leader, and host of the *Memorize Scripture* podcast in which she shares the beauty and power of memorizing scripture.

Angel earned a bachelor's degree in religious studies from California State University, Fullerton. She has received extensive training in youth ministry from Franciscan University of Steubenville and Life Teen and has completed several courses at the Theology of the Body Institute. Throughout her adult life, she has served in many capacities, including youth, young adult, marriage, pro-life, and music ministries. She has released two original music albums, *Your Kingdom Is Glorious* and *Divine Comedy*.

Angel lives in Texas with her husband, Bobby, and their five children.

jackieandbobby.com
Instagram: @jackiefrancois
YouTube: @jackieandbobby